IMAGINING WELFARE

Help

Tom Shakespeare

VENTURE PRESS

BASW website: http://www.basw.co.uk

Published by
VENTURE PRESS
16 Kent Street
Birmingham
B5 6RD

British Library Cataloguing-in-Publication Data
A catalogue record for this book is available from the British Library

ISBN: 1 86178 037 0 (paperback)

Cover design by:
Western Arts
194 Goswell Road
London
EC1V 7DT

Printed in Great Britain

Dedicated to the memory of Pam Carter and Ian Stanton, two Lancastrians who never met, but whose writing, teaching and singing explored difference and equality, powerfully.

CONTENTS

ACKNOWLEDGEMENTS

I would like to thank those who have helped me during the writing of this book. Friends and neighbours on Tyneside have been available when I have needed physical help living with impairment, particularly Lucy Broadhead and Bruce Tuckey, Julia Darling, Clare Satow, Nick Springham, Richard and Barbara Tomlinson. Others have given advice and ideas: Pam Carter, John Clarke, David Colley, Joanna Cox, Mark Erickson, Sharon Gewirtz, Andy Gibson, David Good, Tony Gibson, Helen Groom, Gail Lewis, Ian Parker, Mark Priestley, James Shakespeare, Nick Watson, and members of Newcastle Quaker Meeting. I am particularly grateful to Stuart Bracking, Lynn Froggett, Laura Middleton, Nicholas Sagovsky and Fiona Williams for their comments on the manuscript. Finally, I want to record my debt to those authors to whose work this book owes more than can be conveyed by a simple bibliographical reference: David Brandon, Zygmunt Bauman, Ivan Illich, Bill Jordan, Jenny Morris. The errors, as always, are all mine.

INTRODUCTION

'Help' is one of the shortest and most powerful words in the English language. It describes various acts of assistance. It also constitutes an order or request for people to perform such acts. And, as a call for help, it is a direct appeal for escape or rescue. It is an ambiguous imperative. Because it is both simple and extensive, I have chosen it in preference to the obvious alternative, 'care', in order to describe the areas which are covered in this book. 'Care' is a word which is value-laden, contested and confused, particularly in the way it combines an emotional component and a description of basic human services. There is argument as to when it is necessary, what it means, and how it should be applied. For these reasons, I have tried to avoid it wherever possible.

By 'help', I refer to a range of relationships within the social welfare field. This includes high-status help, such as the work of medical and therapeutic professionals, as well as the low-status help of nurses, social workers and care assistants, and the no-status help of unpaid carers, family and friends. This aid may range from complex intervention such as surgery to basic intervention such as washing. Sometimes it is useful not to draw sharp distinctions between professional and volunteer, or specialist and general help. Drawing distinctions may obscure the fact that all human beings need help on a regular basis. Aristotle suggested that the person who did not need anyone else was either a beast or a god and John Donne wrote that 'No man is an island, sufficient unto himself.' However, I am most interested in the particular kinds of help which are encountered in the health and welfare contexts, and in people who are more likely to receive help and who are often defined in terms of the fact that they are seen to need help in ways which others do not. These people include disabled people, people with learning difficulties, people with mental health problems, older people, people with HIV/AIDS, and children. Of course, there are many differences and distinctions between these very diverse groups. For example, some people are more able than others to make decisions about their lives. Some people need to be supported, while others perhaps need to be kept from harming themselves or others.

Yet, while sensitivity to these differences is very important, there are also significant continuities which justify considering these care-receivers together. Particularly, all these people are subject to social processes of exclusion. In addition to whatever problems they might experience because of their physical or mental condition, in addition to the barriers which are placed in their way by environmental or policy restrictions, people who regularly receive help may be viewed in ways which reinforce their isolation and dependency. They can be seen as objects of care, as patients, as needing protection, as incapable of exercising autonomy, as in-valid. These are strong claims, particularly because modern societies generally pride themselves on the humanity and compassion which vulnerable groups are dealt with. No one wants to believe that children, disabled people or older people are treated badly or cruelly. Yet the facts seem to suggest that this is often the case, and that whether or not direct abuse or neglect occurs, people in these groups are widely devalued. For example, disabled people, older people and children may not be respected or listened to. Even the social policy literature seldom sees things from the point of view of the people who receive help from welfare services. Care-recipients tend to be objectified or ignored within a focus on broader issues about funding, planning and service delivery.

This book discusses the recipient of help, and the way that helping and helpers are experienced. I suggest that 'care' can operate as a kind of imperialism. In the early twentieth century, residential institutions were often actually called 'colonies'. Still today, people who receive welfare or medical help may be taken over, their homes or bodies invaded. In return for help, they have to give up control over their lives. The colonialism incipient in the caring relationship can mean that even the power to define the problem, let alone the way that the problem should be solved, is removed from the person and monopolised by the helper. The help-receiver may be regarded as incapable, incompetent, sometimes even morally inferior – just like attitudes to 'natives' in the former colonies (Memmi, 1990). Receiving help can often lead to various forms of dependency, but this dependency may not be a straightforward outcome of the physical or mental situations which might have led to the need for help, but of the form and the context in which help is provided. Often the need for help is itself an outcome of exclusionary social arrangements, and the outcome of help is further to be rendered dependent and powerless. And things could be otherwise.

The arguments draw on various pieces of qualitative research which I have conducted since 1995. They also refer to some less conventional sources. I have drawn on the imaginative writings of some leading nineteenth-century European authors such as Charles Dickens, Charlotte Brontë, Gustave Flaubert, Franz Kafka, and Anthony Trollope, where they can offer insight into aspects of the helping relationship. Many of the principles and institutions with which we are familiar, date from the Victorian period. This was the time when many charities and the first residential institutions were founded, and when the medical profession began to emerge in its modern form. It was the period when middle-class morality and the role of women as the 'fairer sex' was enshrined. Here, too, notions of disability and dependency were being formed, with distinctions between the deserving and undeserving poor. The work of Charles Dickens is a good example of the insights which fiction can bring to understanding welfare relationships. Themes and situations in his books illustrate the evils of Victorian values very clearly. As a humanitarian, Charles Dickens paints strong pictures of social injustice and devises characters in order to provoke the outrage and shock of his readers. Yet, as a theatrical writer, Dickens cannot help but construct vivid characters drawing on and contributing to stereotype. Often, such characters revolve around disability. These images inform our current discourses of disability and help.

Simon Schama has suggested that the truth which historians seek is nearer to the truth of great novels than of social science. Perhaps conversely, works of fiction can bring insight into issues within social policy and sociology, just as Ken Plummer (1995) has demonstrated how we can understand individual life histories in terms of narrative. John Clarke (1999) has made a strong argument for cultural studies being taken seriously within social policy, and perhaps one aspect of this is to explore the cultural representations of help, charity and dependency which dominate our society. Cultural sources illustrate some of the key themes of the helping relationship. They may also reveal the hidden emotions and transactions within taken-for-granted situations. Here, the book follows the precedent of Jennifer Hockey and Allison James (1993), who also explored issues of dependency in the lives of children, disabled people and older people, looking at issues of cultural metaphor. Social policy has traditionally relied on statistics, and also on the testimonies arising from qualitative research, for communicating a political imperative for welfare reform. Yet imaginative representations may also provide inspiration for rethinking policy and practice. Robert Wuthnow (1991, 179) quotes W.H. Auden's comment: 'You cannot tell people what to do, you can only tell them parables.'

This book is as much four separate essays as one continuous argument. The theme which links the chapters is the idea of colonialism and of the 'other'. '*Helpless*' is about those who receive help, and the social treatment and cultural constructions which render them excluded. '*Helpers*' is about people who give help, including professionals, volunteers and relatives. '*Helping*' looks at the relationship between '*Helpers*' and help-recipients itself, particularly in its institutional forms. '*Helpful*' suggests alternative approaches which may resolve some of the problems.

Chapter 1
HELPLESS

This chapter explores cultural representations of disability and dependency. We are used to thinking of disability in individual and medical terms. But our understandings of what it means to be disabled, or to receive care, draw on broader social constructions: they are not 'natural' or inevitable. Just as 'the family' or 'a homosexual' are concepts which can only be understood in specific historical situations, so terms such as 'child', 'disabled person' and 'the elderly' do not label distinct biological processes, but emerge in cultural contexts and mean different things in different times and places. Understanding the dominance of particular stereotypes of disability and discourses of dependency in modern thinking can demonstrate how these experiences can best be understood in terms of structures of meaning and collective values.

A particular theme in the following discussion is the way that people who are physically or mentally different are seen as 'Other'. This notion conveys the idea that disabled people are seen as abnormal and alien. The notion of otherness is explored through images of disability in novels. Next, there is an outline of the processes involved in the metaphor of disability and otherness. There follows a discussion of discourses of care and dependency within social policy, to show how these also reinforce the otherness of care-recipients. The chapter ends with an exploration of alternative approaches to disability and dependency.

Disability and dependency in culture
Representations of disability can be found in a wide range of cultural sources, ranging from mythology and folklore to contemporary Hollywood films. In Greek and Roman plays, the villains had red hair and we might remember that 'sinister' is Latin for 'left', connecting left-handed people with evil. But there are also more complex uses of impairment, for example in the plays of Sophocles. The tragic hero Oedipus, after his crimes of patricide and incest, ends up blinded at Colonnus. But his status as a disabled character predates this fate. Oedipus' father, having heard the prophecy of his fate, deliberately wounds his young son, who is crippled as a result ('Oedipus' means swollen foot). Disability here seems to symbolise the tragic flaw. Philoctetes has a similar impairment. He is an important fighter in the army that goes to Troy, particularly because of his magic bow. The Greeks go to make a sacrifice, which is interrupted because one of the temple snakes bites Philoctetes on the foot. The wound becomes infected and nauseatingly smelly. His companions

abandon him on an island, where he is marooned for ten years, while they attempt unsuccessfully to defeat the Trojans. Finally, they realise that they have to return and fetch Philoctetes: he and his magic bow are essential to their victory. Sophocles' play symbolises the idea that disabled people have qualities which make up for their lack, but it is also a commentary on the prejudice, isolation and exploitation which a disabled person might experience.

As the contrasting tales of Oedipus and Philoctetes demonstrate, stereotypes of disability can be used in different ways: sometimes a minor character has an impairment to heighten an atmosphere of exoticism or difference; sometimes a major character has an impairment to illustrate a particular personality trait; sometimes the impairment may be a necessary aspect of the plot. Disabled people may be represented as sinister and twisted (Shakespeare's Richard III or Robert Louis Stevenson's Blind Pew), or as pathetic innocents, and sometimes as superhuman and possessing compensatory abilities. Whether superficially positive or negative, these images are usually exploitative and one-dimensional, reinforcing popular prejudices about disability rather than creating rounded and realistic characters. As Rosemarie Garland Thomson (1997) argues, they are stylised and overdetermined: impairment dominates over other character attributes. Yet images and constructions of disability and dependency are never coherent, and are usually drawing on contradictory ideas. So, for example, people with learning difficulties can be seen as simultaneously helpless and threatening, and both asexual and sexually dangerous and polluting. The rest of this section draws on various novels of the nineteenth and early twentieth centuries, in order to explore how disability is represented. These books, of course, are not about gods or heroes, but are about ordinary people. Modern ideas about normality and abnormality were shaped in this period and influenced by these discourses.

Charles Dickens was particularly fond of giving a character an impairment, often to heighten a sense of pathos, or make them seem more ridiculous or evil. For example, several characters in *Our Mutual Friend* (1864–5) are distinguished in this way. Silas Wegg is a self-important and ultimately treacherous minor character, whose main role is to exploit his benefactor.

> *'Wegg was a knotty man, and a close-grained, with a face carved out of very hard material, that had just as much play of expression as a watchman's rattle. When he laughed, certain jerks occurred in it, and the rattle sprung. Sooth to say, he was so wooden a man that he seemed to have taken his wooden leg naturally, and rather suggested to the fanciful observer, that he might be expected – if his development received no*

untimely check – to be completely set up with a pair of wooden legs in about six months.' (Dickens, 1985a, 89)

Wegg's impairment defines his personality. One might even imagine that the name, 'Wegg', was just a contraction of the identifier, 'wooden leg'. By giving him a wooden leg, Dickens makes him distinctive and more ridiculous and perhaps even more sinister. One remembers Long John Silver and Captain Ahab, other obsessed and revengeful characters of nineteenth-century fiction: although while they are dark and tragic, Silas Wegg remains in the realm of farce (along with Captain Hook). A more central character in the same book is Bradley Headstone, the schoolteacher: the story of his self-destructive and obsessive passion for Lizzie Hexham is a key part of the narrative. In order to contribute to our view of the man as driven and passionate and dangerous, Dickens describes him as having an epileptic seizure on discovering that Lizzie is to marry his bitter rival, Eugene Wrayburn. While Wegg is comically conniving, and Headstone is passionately brutal, Dickens's darkest disabled character is Quilp, in *The Old Curiosity Shop* (1840–1):

'The child was closely followed by an elderly man of remarkably hard features and forbidding aspect, and so low in stature as to be quite a dwarf, though his head and face were large enough for the body of a giant. His black eyes were restless, sly and cunning; his mouth and chin, bristly with the stubble of coarse hard beard; and his complexion was one of that kind which never looks clean or wholesome. But what added most to the grotesque expression of his face, was a ghastly smile, which, appearing to be the mere result of habit and to have no connection with any mirthful or complacent feeling, constantly revealed the few dis-coloured fangs that were yet scattered in his mouth, and gave him the aspect of a panting dog.' (Dickens, 1985b, 65)

Unsurprisingly, these physical characteristics are accompanied by negative personality traits: Quilp is lecherous, avaricious and malign. He represents all the malevolent aspects of the mythological dwarf.

A competing stereotype is of the tragic innocent, most often a disabled child. Looking again at the work of Charles Dickens, the character of Tiny Tim in *A Christmas Carol* (1843) is an obvious example of this highly sentimental use of disability. So is Little Nell, in *The Old Curiosity Shop*. Another such use comes with the pauper child Johnny in *Our Mutual Friend*, whose only role in the book is to fall ill and die, while in the process being generally loving and loveable and pathetic. In Charlotte Brontë's novel, *Jane Eyre* (1847), the con-sumptive schoolfriend Helen Burns plays a similar role: although increasingly affected by tuberculosis, she is always brave and noble, and an ally to Jane at the dreadful orphan school. On her deathbed she displays all the Christian virtues of faith and goodness, bravely welcoming death at the age of 14 because it will mean she avoids further suffering and is united with her Maker.

The character of Smike, in Dickens's *Nicholas Nickleby*, is an older variant of the innocent disabled person, although he seems to have learning difficulties rather than a physical impairment:

> *'The poor soul was poring hard over a tattered book, with the traces of recent tears still upon his face; vainly endeavouring to master some task which a child of nine years old, possessed of ordinary powers, could have conquered with ease, but which, to the addled brain of the crushed boy of nineteen, was a sealed and hopeless mystery.'* (Dickens, 1978, 143–4)

His appearance is ridiculous: an emaciated teenager, he is dressed in the clothes of a child. Dickens's descriptions reinforce the picture of Smike as a tragic disabled person: he is 'timid, broken-spirited', a 'poor, half-witted creature' who is 'wretched' and 'careworn'. The simple, pathetic Smike is devoted to Nicholas, who is the only person who stands up for him against the wicked Mr Squeers, and he follows Nicholas around until finally and inevitably he dies – although, like Helen Burns, he welcomes death because it takes him away from suffering to a glorious Heavenly existence.

Characters like Helen Burns and Smike exist to point up the horrors of social conditions in the orphan schools and institutions of Victorian England: they are tragic but brave disabled people who are designed to arouse indignation and pity in the reader. Yet, the political critique is achieved at the cost of reinforcing a negative image of disability. Such characters can also provide an object lesson to the novel's hero or heroine, or else the opportunity for the lead character to prove their own merit and kindness. Rosemarie Garland Thomson, in discussing American social reform novels such as *Uncle Tom's Cabin*, suggests that these types of disabled character define and legitimate the role of maternal benefactress for middle-class women, who were at that time socially excluded from other roles in society. Perhaps Dickens is satirising this tendency when the newly enriched Mrs Boffin, in *Our Mutual Friend*, chooses the pauper child Johnny to adopt and look after.

Jane Eyre exploits disability as a plot device. The heroine comes to work for Mr Rochester as governess to his adopted child. The secret presence in the house of Mr Rochester's first wife creates dramatic tension. First the only evidence of her presence are sounds that Jane hears in the night: 'It was a curious laugh; distinct, formal, mirthless.' (Brontë,1977, 131). She also hears eccentric murmurs, gurgling and moaning, and is woken by a 'demoniac laugh – low, suppressed and deep' (1977, 175) and later by a scream which is compared with that of a wild bird of prey. Later, the mysterious woman bites and sucks the blood of her victims. Jane compares her to a vampire, and is shocked at the sight of her: '*I never saw a face like it! It was a discoloured face – it was a savage face. I wish I could forget the roll of the red eyes and the fearful blackened inflation of the lineaments!*' (1977, 322). The first Mrs Rochester fulfils the evil stereotype; as her husband later acknowledges: '*Bertha Mason is mad; and she came of a mad family; idiots and maniacs through three generations! Her mother, the Creole, was both a mad woman and a drunkard!*' (1977, 331).

Here, notions of racial exoticism add to the sense of otherness and threat: the Caribbean woman who had first seemed dark and exotic turns out to be mad, bad and dangerous too. Bertha Rochester heightens the melodrama and mystery; she also operates as a stereotyped disabled character; finally, her role is central to the plot. The revelation of her existence leads to the critical denouement halfway through the novel, following which Jane Eyre has to leave Mr Rochester. Later, Bertha destroys Rochester's home in the fire which leads to his own disabling injuries and her death, but also ultimately to the novel's happy conclusion.

In *Lady Chatterley's Lover*, by D.H. Lawrence (1960), the war injury of Sir Clifford Chatterley sets up the entire plot, in which his wife is transformed by the sexual relationship she develops with Mellors, the gamekeeper, but it is also central to the metaphorical life of the story. The novel is primarily about sexuality and about class: disability is the catalyst for the affair, rather than of interest in its own right. However, Sir Clifford's impairment symbolises his general incapacity to love, or to understand women, or to be a real man. Throughout the book he is infantilised. For example, while he has manual and powered wheelchairs, '*Yet he was absolutely dependent on her, he needed her every moment. Big and strong as he was, he was helpless. . . . But alone he was like a lost thing*' (1960,17). He is described as a 'child man', his impotence contrasted with the passionate sexual energy of the working man. Moreover, he is unable to have authentic feelings: he has the 'slight vacancy of the cripple.' (1960, 6). All of his negative character traits are connected, we are led to understand, with his injury. In a powerful scene, Sir Clifford's motor chair cannot ascend an incline on his estate, and he has to ask Mellors to push: the discussion of the broken motor and its rods and gears is clearly a direct metaphor for the disabled man's physical lack, not just of legs but also of functioning penis.

The notion of disability robbing a man of his masculinity is a common trope, particularly in postwar Hollywood films – for example, *The Men*, *Born on the Fourth of July*, and even *Forrest Gump*. But in this novel, D.H. Lawrence uses Chatterley's impairment highly specifically, to symbolise his own hatred of what industrial capital was doing to Britain, and the failure of the bourgeois man to respect or understand the 'real men' of the working class.

Dickens, Brontë and Lawrence were not interested in disability as such. Instead, their disabled characters function metaphorically: either to manipulate the emotions of the reader, or to enable the author to develop plot or convey a deeper symbolism. For this reason, although often vivid and memorable, such characters can be rather shallow and two-dimensional. Usually, the disabled character is defined by their impairment, and remains an object, rather than a subject exercising agency in their own right: things are done to them, rather than them doing things. It is also important to draw attention to the way in which normality is constructed in opposition to these images of dependency and impairment. From his analyses, Lennard Davis concludes that disability is a key element of the novel as a artistic form:

> *'In thinking through the issue of disability, I have come to see that almost any literary work will have some reference to the abnormal, to disability, and so on. I would explain this phenomenon as a result of the hegemony of normalcy. This normalcy must be constantly enforced in public venues (like the novel), must always be creating and bolstering its image by processing, comparing, constructing, deconstructing images of normalcy and the abnormal.'* (Davis, 1997, 23)

The meaning of the disability metaphor

We have discovered that images of disability are relatively common (they are as ubiquitous in Hollywood cinema as they are in Victorian novels), and that while they encompass a range of stereotypes, they are centrally about metaphor, rather than about the realistic experience of impairment itself. Cultural texts can both reflect and influence our ideas about real life. Stereotypes of disability work for the reader because we can fill in the gaps: they reproduce ideas or preconceptions with which we are familiar. As children grow up, they learn about disabled people partly through the books and films and legends which they encounter, and so real disabled people are understood in terms of fictional stereotypes. Consider the 'triumph over tragedy' stories which dominate the media, or the 'supercrip' image which accounts for our fascination with Helen Keller or Stephen Hawking or Evelyn Glennie. Professionals or the public do not learn how to treat disabled people from

Shakespeare's plays or James Bond films, but the discourses of disability which we have identified contribute to a cultural undertow of prejudice, which contributes towards policy and practice.

The American historian Paul Longmore argues that it is fear of disability which underlies media stereotypes:

> *'What we fear, we often stigmatise and shun and sometimes seek to destroy. Popular entertainments depicting disabled characters allude to these fears and prejudices or address them obliquely or fragmentarily, seeking to reassure us about ourselves.'* (Longmore, 1987, 66)

This insight highlights the way that representations of disability may often be more about reinforcing normality than an interest in disability itself. Impairment becomes something which other people have, and which is not part of ordinary embodiment. As Jenny Morris has argued,

> *'Surely, the representation and exploration of human experience is incomplete as long as disability is either missing from or misrepresented in all the forms that cultural representation takes. It is fear and denial of the frailty, vulnerability, mortality and* arbitrariness *of human experience that deters us from confronting such realities. Fear and denial prompts the isolation of those who are disabled, ill, or old as "Other", as "not like us".'* (emphasis original) (Morris, 1991, 85)

Morris and Longmore are suggesting that cultural representations reinforce or speak to a tendency for non-disabled people to exclude people with impairment, and to define themselves in opposition to them. One group – those with 'normal' bodies – is legitimated, while another group – those with 'in-valid' or deviant bodies – is seen as inferior and abnormal. This process is called 'Othering', and can be demonstrated to occur between men and women, heterosexuals and homosexuals, and between members of dominant ethnic groups and minority ethnic groups.

My analysis of disabled people, children, older people and other groups as helpless and excluded builds on a tradition of theorising the Other. Simone de Beauvoir (1976), writing about the way men define themselves in opposition to women, and Albert Memmi (1990), writing about colonised peoples, have shown how relations of domination construct the Other as object, but also as lack and void and mystery, not individualised but anonymous and generalised (Hartsock, 1990, 160). The critic Edward Said (1994) has shown how the nineteenth- and early twentieth-century literature constructs and reinforces colonialism, even when it appears to be talking about something else, producing the Orient as the phobic projection of a western imaginary. Disabled critics have argued that the same process is happening in terms of disability. Ludmilla Jordanova has summarised what Othering involves:

> *'The idea of Otherness is complicated, but certain themes are common: the treatment of the Other as more like an object, something to be managed and possessed, and as dangerous, wild, threatening. At the same time, the Other becomes an entity whose very separateness inspires curiosity, invites enquiring knowledge. The Other is to be veiled and unveiled.'* (Jordanova, 1989, 110)

The dominant group both separates itself from the Other, but also depends on the Other for the sense of its own identity. To be a man is to avoid effeminacy or dependency, or woman-identified behaviours and activities. The definition of able-bodied is non-disabled. Frantz Fanon (1986) explores the ways in which this uneasy relationship involves resentment, envy and aggression. Domination leads the Other to have feelings of inferiority and neuroses as a result of traumatising contact with the dominant world. The white gaze annihilates body and individuality as the black person becomes no more than their skin colour and may end up wanting to become white, and, in the same way, some disabled people long for a cure. Able-bodiedness (whiteness) is the criterion for beauty and acceptability.

The separation into able-bodied and disabled is an artificial process, one which is policed and reinforced by the imagery of Othering. In fact, everyone is impaired: everyone has a body which is imperfect and flawed, susceptible to illness and disease, subject to ageing and inevitably mortal. The idea that the world neatly divides into people with physical limitations and 'normal' people who have perfect bodies is an illusion. Only by projecting their frailty and vulnerability onto the Other – old people, disabled people – can non-disabled people maintain the illusion of their own strength and wholeness. To be able-bodied is to be in denial. This suggests the truth of Jenny Morris's claim:

> *'Our disability frightens people. They don't want to think that this is something which could happen to them. So we become separated from common humanity, treated as fundamentally different and alien. Having put up clear barriers between us and them, non-disabled people further hide their fear and discomfort by turning us into objects of pity, comforting themselves by their own kindness and generosity.'* (Morris, 1991, 192)

The cultural stereotypes of disability discussed earlier serve to amplify and mark out disabled people as different, as outside the normal run of things, as alien. Disabled people are scapegoats for the fears and vulnerabilities of non-disabled people – what David Hevey has called 'dustbins for disavowal' (Hevey, 1992, 34).

This discussion has begun to uncover the origins of disabling imagery, and to account for the vast range of stereotypical characters found in western culture. It is my claim that these representations show the importance of disability for non-disabled artists and audiences, and reveal the processes of Othering and anomaly which enable the 'normal' population to maintain a sense of themselves and also deal with the existence of minority groups such as older people, disabled people, and people with mental illness or learning difficulties. Fundamentally, representations present such 'helpless' people as the outcome of natural processes, not social exclusion. These images are central to culture and the media, and contribute to the environment in which children learn about the world. It would be surprising if they did not also influence discourses on health and welfare.

Disability and dependency in social policy
In this section, I trace four dimensions of the academic and policy literature on social care which could be said to continue the processes introduced above. In the images and analyses which we have encountered, disabled people have been firmly marked out as different from non-disabled people; they have been objectified; they have been represented as tragic but brave, or sinister and evil, or as possessing compensatory abilities, but never as ordinary and normal. Unfortunately, variants of these tendencies can be uncovered in the professional literature. Those who become reliant on professional help become viewed as dependent:

> *'Because neediness is conceived as a threat to autonomy, those who have more needs than us appear to be less autonomous, and hence less powerful and less capable. The result is that one way in which we socially construct those who need care is to think of them as pitiful because they require help.'* (Tronto, 1993, 120)

The following discussion explores these tendencies in the social policy literature on disabled people, older people, and children.

1. Polarisation
Discourses on disability reflect and reinforce the opposition between normality and abnormality. But this is an artificial distinction and an exaggeration. There are not two 'natural' categories of dependent and independent. Everyone is impaired, and all people have areas of vulnerability. No one is

more than 'temporarily able-bodied'. Independence is a myth. Moreover, disabled people can be successful and high-achieving and powerful, despite our habits of thought. The life of F.D. Roosevelt is an example of the way that disability is seen as incompatible with power. He had contracted polio in 1921, and ever afterwards used a wheelchair to get about. He could not stand without support. Yet as President of the United States of America, he had to represent the idea of a strong and independent nation: he could not be seen to be weak or dependent. In the popular imagination, you cannot be disabled and dominant. There are approximately 35,000 photographs of the President in existence. Only two unpublished photographs show him in his wheelchair (Gallagher, 1985).

Yet no one is really independent. The human being has evolved over millennia to be more dependent. For example, of all animals, humans have the longest period of infancy and the most extreme infant dependency. Yet this period of social and intellectual learning is essential for humans to achieve advanced culture, language and civilisation. Human dependency in childhood is a direct evolutionary outcome of success in adulthood (O'Hear, 1997) . Moreover, no adult is really independent. Everyone depends on others, whether to drive the bus or deliver milk, or perform any number of basic personal and systemic maintenance roles. We are all service users. Mike Oliver suggests:

> *'No one in a modern industrial society is completely independent, for we live in a state of mutual interdependence. The dependence of disabled people, therefore, is not a feature which marks them out as different in kind from the rest of the population but as different in degree.'* (Oliver, 1993, 50)

In fact, it has been a tradition that the more dependent you are, in some circumstances, the higher status you have. For example, if you describe a family who live in segregated accommodation, are looked after and have their meals cooked for them, go to special schools, do not look after their own money, have people to drive them around, and are likely to be stared at wherever they go, it might be imagined you were talking about a very dependent type of person. Yet you could be describing the British Royal Family.

The implication is that the usual way of defining dependent people as having 'special needs' might also be prejudice, rather than reality. Why do disabled people have special needs? Disabled people need the same things as everyone else: they need housing, education, employment, information and services. In fact, disabled people have ordinary needs, which are not normally met. The result is that they have to rely on particular kinds of helping services which are seen as rendering them abnormal and inferior. The problem lies not in the individual, but in the services and environments which render the disabled person excluded and needy.

2. The burden of dependants

People who receive care may become conceptualised as dependent. Warnes (1993) argues, with reference to the treatment of older people, that there is a tendency to objectify those people who receive welfare services. Making a comparison with Jonathan Swift's notorious *Modest Proposal*, Warnes counsels against the mindset of burden becoming or remaining a characteristic of social policy or political analysis, even by those with progressive intentions:

> *'What happens is that the agents carrying the burdens are misidentified: the more graphic the portrayal of the wearisomeness of old age, poverty or sickness, the greater the sense of grievous load upon others. Sometimes the distortion is so great that, following Swift's modest proposal, it turns out that those who experience the burden are of so little concern that they become disposable.'* (Warnes, 1993, 329)

In the case of older people, the experience of old age is essentialised and problematised, as if older people were invariably incapable and physically dependent (Phillipson *et al.*, 1986). This pathology model of old age ignores the many older people who continue to be successful and non-needy. Images of older people focus either on a jolly grandparent stereotype or on a desolate and frail person. During the nineteenth century, the word 'senile' changed its meaning, from merely 'old' to 'deteriorated and incapable'. Doctors in the twentieth century have medicalised old age by defining it as pathological. In social policy, emotive words about the 'demographic timebomb' and the burden of an ageing population serve to undermine the individuality and agency of older people:

> *'Phrases such as "the growing burden of elderly people" or "the rising tide of elderly mentally frail people" have themselves entered into the theory and practice of social work, distorting both the nature of the social work response and the worker's relationship with older people.'* (Phillipson, 1989, 193)

Such references are used both to justify restrictions in social expenditure and to suggest that an ageing population is both unnatural and undesirable.

Jens Qvortrup (1990) has criticised the exclusion of children from most statistics and social accounting: young people are invisible in the way in which married women used to be. He suggests that there is an unquestioned child dependency within this documentation, a protective exclusion from public life.

In fact, often children are conceived of in terms of a cost. This may be a financial cost on their parents, or as an item on 'time-budget' studies. Having parenting or caring commitments, then, is represented in terms of the burden of children. The social policy debate on provision of childcare and the possibilities of women entering the workforce similarly regards children as a burden, or a problem to be solved.

The discourse of burden also applies to disabled people who are placed in situations where their children have to take up a caring role. The literature on young carers, exploring situations where children take on caring roles in relation to parents with impairments, tends to objectify disabled parents as 'dependants', and to characterise the situation as a 'plight' or 'curse'. A positive attempt to challenge the social exclusion of child carers slips all too easily into a tendency to pathologise people with impairments who choose to have children (Olsen, 1996; Olsen and Parker, 1997, 127). The children of disabled people are seen as victims: '*This carries the danger of implicit and explicit criticism of disabled parents, their values, their choices, and even their right to have children at all*' (Olsen, 1996, 42). By focusing on the single issue of young carers, this research can obscure other issues: for example, it may ignore the fact that disabled people can be carers. In problematising families with a disabled parent, there is a danger of ignoring the ways in which all families involve interdependence: for example, older children looking after younger children, and other age-appropriate responsibilities for children (Keith and Morris, 1994, 53). In general, the accounts of families with a disabled person as mother or father are guilty of essentialising and pathologising disability, and suggesting that disabled people cannot make good parents and that their children become the victims of this incompetence and selfishness, all on the basis of very scant research.

The literature on disabled children similarly has tended to rely on the assumption that having a child with impairment is to experience inevitable burden, for example in the titles of older books on the subject such as *A Constant Burden*. Emotive and offensive terms like 'severely disabled' implicitly blame the victim for their situation. The literature tends to make a range of normative assumptions about the effects of having a child with impairment on the parental relationship or the family dynamics: for example, a suggestion that having a disabled child means that relationships break down, or that siblings suffer. There tends to be a suggestion that, in the case of a child with impairment, the typical loving parental relationships are replaced by a relationship of caring and physical support based around performance of certain tasks.

Services provided for families with disabled children reflect this assumption of burden: there is a considerable stress on the need for respite care, for example, on the basis that the heavy responsibilities of having a child with impairment typically necessitate a break or a rest. The same 'intolerable burden' model of respite care is evident in policies relating to adults with learning difficulties (Cotterill *et al.*, 1997) which tend to stress the benefits to the carer, rather than any positive outcomes for the service user. Yet parents themselves may be most anxious about the desires and experiences of the cared-for person. Again, practice literature on fostering and adoption stresses the special qualities needed to look after disabled children, and the particular problems which carers of disabled children have to deal with, in ways which sometimes make disabled children sound like sacks of potatoes, or exotic zoo animals. The emphasis of many policies is on the needs and wishes of parents and siblings: it is rare that disabled children themselves are asked what they think about them.

Broader debates in the area of social policy also reflect the tendency to view disabled people as an inevitable burden on their families, and to biologise and individualise the problem of disablement. The carer movement has redefined care in a way which enshrines this notion of burden, as I will argue in the next chapter. Again,. Morris (1991) has drawn attention to the work of feminists such as Finch, Groves and Dalley, whose critique of the ways in which women perform the majority of care in the community led to their demand for more residential care, a view which ignores the views and rights of disabled people and other recipients of care. The irony of the literature focusing on women as carers is that it fails to notice that women are also disabled people.

Another area of literature which constructs an argument of disabled people (especially children) as burdens is the discussion of pre-natal screening and termination of foetuses affected by congenital impairment. This discourse rests on a number of assumptions: that being a disabled person involves a life of suffering; that disabled people are inevitably dependent on others; that the state will ultimately have to bear the cost of supporting disabled people. Public health writers such as Nicholas Wald make explicit the ways in which screening programmes are evaluated on the basis of cost–benefit analysis regarding the avoidance of the burden of disabled children (Wald *et al.*, 1992).

3. Lack of a voice
Also evident in the literature is the way in which people who receive care are denied a voice: whether the discussion is about older people, disabled people, children or people with HIV/AIDS, it is not common for first-hand accounts to be available. We therefore rely for our information on the projections of policy-

makers and academics or professionals, or sometimes the testimonies of non-disabled relatives and carers. For example, it is very rare to hear directly from the disabled child in literature on disabled childhood (Shakespeare and Watson, 1998). Baldwin and Carlisle, in their review of the literature, tell us *'We lack children's accounts of pain, discomfort, dependence on Other for feeding, bathing and toileting. We do not know how they feel about the way doctors, social workers, therapists and other children treat them.'* (1994, 35).

People with learning difficulties have traditionally been assumed to be unable to speak for themselves, and their voices have been eclipsed by those of family members or professionals. The rise of the self-advocacy movement, in the form of groups which are often called 'Speaking up . . .' or 'Speaking for ourselves', challenges this silencing. Research has shown the ways in which case histories of people with learning difficulties tend to silence them. The notes do not give family details, or record the achievements of people with learning difficulties. They contain clinical information, or details of value to the professional, not to the person themselves:

> *'Lack of personal history material within official records appears to create a vacuum all too easily filled by a "professional" version, namely a "case history". The privileging of professional histories maintains the membership of people with learning difficulties within a marginalised and stigmatised group and confirms their identity as "cases", rather than individuals.'* (Gillman *et al.*, 1997, 683)

This approach can be contrasted with a life history approach, which enables people to be seen as active agents, as normal members of society, as people who have a life.

As other analysts have shown, we do not hear from the person who is cared for in the literature on caring, whether it is the feminist literature on community care, or the new literature on children as carers. Thus Jenny Morris criticises Gillian Dalley's models of collective residential care for failing to let disabled people's voices be heard (1991, 157). There has been criticism of researchers using terms which respondents are unwilling to use themselves, for example, where the 'young carers' researchers are accused of imposing their own definitions and per-ceptions on the subjects of their research (Keith and Morris, 1994, 39). In fact, the rise of carer literature displaces the voices of the cared-for even further (Keith and Morris, 1994, 37), just as in the political and policy arena the development of a carers' movement challenges the gains of disabled people's organisations. Warnes argues that the construction of the debate itself implies the submergence of the service-recipient's voice: *'the focus on care-giver burden by definition gives a primary position to the provider of care'* (1993 326).

The failure to hear the voices of those who receive care means that the problematic aspects of the experience for them are sometimes neglected. For example, the family may be the site of oppression for disabled people (Morris, 1991, 143). This may be to do with the paternalism or over protectiveness of parents towards children with impairments. Alternatively, it is clear that there is a high prevalence of abuse of disabled children, and also of older people, which is attributable to the role of care within the family, as well as to the behaviour of people outside the family. These issues will be highlighted in the next chapter. I am not suggesting that we should not listen to or research the experiences of carers. However, it is a priority to consider and research the voices of people placed into a situation of dependency or having impairments, rather than to use carers, parents or professionals as proxies. Of course, we must consider the civil rights of parents and carers, but this can only happen on the basis of the full and prior consideration of the civil rights of disabled people and older people.

4. Infantilisation
We have seen the polarity between normal and abnormal people; the tendency to view the latter as a burden; and the failure to hear the voices of care-receivers. Some people have suggested that a broader process is occurring, whereby recipients of care are regarded as if they were children, just as, in the colonial era, the colonised were seen as childlike and immature, in need of civilising discipline. The sociologist Jens Qvortrup argues that the distinction between adults and children is an organising principle of modern societies. A polarity between dependent, vulnerable, innocent, asexual children and competent, powerful, sexual, adult citizens is central to our ways of thinking.

At first sight, adults who are disabled or mentally ill or old or have learning difficulties seem to challenge this polarity. Yet often a major part of the stigma experienced by these different adults is to be treated as if they were children: they are to be protected, they are incompetent, they are to be 'seen and not heard', they require others to make decisions for them, they cannot work or live independently, or be sexual. In short, they are not normal adult citizens.

Jenny Hockey and Allison James discuss the humiliating effects of this kind of discourse in what they call 'the metaphoric role of childhood' in framing dependency. Older people may be particularly subject to this infantilisation. We are familiar with terms like 'second childhood', and affectionate but patronising phrases such as 'little old lady' and 'old boy' and 'old girl'. They argue that related processes occur in the treatment of disabled and chronically sick people. Hockey and James conclude:

> *'Infantilisation processes can have a powerful and potent role in shaping many dependent people's everyday experiences, engendering feelings of social marginalization, personal humiliation and emotional vulnerability.'*
> (Hockey and James, 1993, 10)

Most non-disabled adults do not experience these processes. However, women have traditionally been treated as childlike, as Shulamith Firestone argued (1979). Although this has mainly changed with the advent of a more sexually egalitarian society, women attending antenatal clinics still enter into a curious process of infantilisation:

> *'The passivity required of a mother in medicalised childbirth is a microcosm of the passivity associated with femininity. For example, the advice and instruction given by midwives, nurses and health visitors can undermine the mother's status as an adult.'* (Hugman, 1991, 193)

This suggests that the perceived need for medical care and supervision can temporarily displace the usual adult role. It also points to the particular dynamics of the doctor/patient relationship which will be explored further in the next chapter.

The cultural models of dependency which have been considered here also relate to material and economic processes. It is no coincidence that most of the groups under discussion have been non-productive, in a market sense, since the early industrial revolution. Many disabled people, most older people and children do not work. In our society, paid work is a major marker of status. Those groups which are excluded from the market are consequently devalued. The changing status of women, since the early 1970s, can perhaps be linked to the fact that women are entering paid work more than ever before. Where people are not allowed to make an economic and social contribution, or where their contribution is not recognised, then their position in a capitalist society is likely to remain marginal.

Redefining the problem

We have seen how cultural representations and social policy analysis can fall into the same errors. These stem from a tendency to take dependency for granted, and see it as a natural outcome of having an impairment, or growing old. Added to these assumptions are tendencies to treat people who receive care as abnormal, as alien, as burdens, and as childlike. This book is an attempt to challenge these approaches, and to reconfigure our understandings of disability and dependency. Prevailing approaches to dependency are flawed because they rest on a model which both individualises and medicalises the experience of disability or ageing. It is as seen as automatic that older people or disabled people or people with HIV/AIDS need care. The problem of disability is located in the deficits of an individual who does not operate in the usual way, whether because of physical or mental incapacity. Yet many commentators and campaigners have suggested that it is more helpful to locate these problems in a collective and social and structural context. Dependency is a production of particular social relations.

One dimension of the traditional model is that the wider environment and the role it plays in creating social dependency is ignored. For example, if a house is inaccessible, or is located far from public transport, or on the top of a hill, there will be consequences for a person with impairment or physical limitation. These disabling factors could be avoided if the person was housed in a barrier-free setting. If someone lives in a city with inaccessible transport, they will be dependent on an ambulance or a taxi or a volunteer to a greater extent than if they lived in an accessible city. Equally, if a disabled person did not face physical and attitudinal barriers to employment, they would be more likely to get a job and therefore escape dependency on benefits.

People are disabled by society, as well as by their bodies. It is the social and environmental barriers, prejudicial attitudes and other exclusionary processes which often make living with an impairment so hard for disabled people and their families. Cultural representations of disability, and professional discourses of welfare dependency, are another way in which people are disabled. This approach, known as the social model, emerged from the campaigns of the disabled people's movement. It can enable us to look at care debates in a new light. However, it can be applied more broadly to explore the processes of oppression and marginalisation which apply to members of other help-receiving groups.

'It is not physical impairment which is the barrier to asserting choice and control. Rather, it is the obstacles which society constructs: the over-protectiveness of professionals and parents; the undermining of self-esteem; the failure of non-disabled people to develop appropriate communication skills.' (Morris, 1993, 173)

Keith and Morris (1994, p.45ff.) focus attention on the factors which make a disabled parent reliant on the personal assistance of a young carer. These include poverty, disabling professional attitudes, disabling services, disabling environments and the broader problems of disabling experiences and disabling communities. Disabled parents rely on their children as carers not because they wish to, but because society has failed to provide them with adequate social support. A social model of disability relocates the problem of dependency from being a corollary of impairment to being a product of a disabling society. Rather than putting resources into support for young carers, it would be appropriate to put resources into integrated living schemes and personal assistance, which would render dependence on child carers unnecessary.

When Keith and Morris make the following comment about child carers, it is equally relevant to the debate about disabled children: *'The choice both parent and child have in these circumstances is often dependent on access to external support, accessible housing and appropriate aids and equipment'* (1994, 54). Rather than seeing the problems of disabled childhood as a result of the child's impairment, it is beneficial to look at the wider context of support and services extended to different families. This point is made by parents in Bryony Beresford's research on *Positively Parents* (1994): there were many responses suggesting that it was not the impairment itself which was the main problem for the family, but poverty and the reactions of others. Many of the experiences of families with disabled children did not differ qualitatively from those of families with non-disabled children, many of which are also isolated and impoverished. As Beresford concludes:

> *'We should not forget, therefore, that a parent caring for a disabled child may also be facing other stresses which, to them, may be far more problematic than those associated with the disabled child.'* (Beresford, 1994, 111)

The social model parallels the work within social gerontology on the structured dependency of old age (Townsend, 1981). This approach attributes the problems of ageing not to individual or medical deficits, but to the decline in financial resources of older people in the postwar period; to compulsory retirement; to passivity-inducing community care; and to the way that the expansion in residential provision has led to a reduction in support for people in their own homes. Estes argues:

> *'The needs of older persons are reconceptualised as deficiencies by the professionals charged with treating them, regardless of whether the origins of these needs lie in social conditions over which the individual has little or no control, in the failings of the individual, or in some policymaker's decision that a need exists.'* (Estes, 1979, 235)

The social focus of research and policy is on individual adjustment to ageing, not the social arrangements which disempower and marginalise older people.

Even old people themselves are made to feel incapable and limited. Moreover there is a lack of priority and prestige given to working with older people within social work, health and social research itself.

Since the early 1980s, the social sciences have deconstructed discourses on gender and race and sexuality to demonstrate that what was always thought to be 'natural' are actually the products of social and cultural processes. The positions of disabled people, older people and children are now at last being reconsidered along similar lines. The implications for helping will be considerable.

Conclusion

In challenging the images of dependency which are communicated in literature or within contemporary care practices, it is necessary to develop an appreciation of the ordinariness and agency of disabled people and older people. Rather than treating those who receive care as alien beings, imprisoned in failed bodies, the role of society in creating and constructing the problem of helplessness has to be acknowledged. This may also be important for those who are on the receiving end of help, who may have internalised their idea of their own incapacity, and may expect no better than the treatment and attitudes which they experience. As Paolo Freire has written:

> *'Self-depreciation is another characteristic of the oppressed, which derives from their internalisation of the opinion the oppressors hold of them. So often do they hear that they are good for nothing, know nothing, and are incapable of learning anything – that they are sick, lazy and unproductive – that in the end they become convinced of their own unfitness.'* (Freire, 1972, 38)

Just as colonialism has historically led to the corruption and degradation of indigenous cultures, so the impact of colonial care may be to undermine the self-respect and positivity of those rendered dependent, and to create constituencies who are to an extent psychically damaged by the treatment they have received. This is the subject which Fanon has illuminated: there is an urgent task, beyond the current discussion, to explore the healing which is essential amongst those at the margins of the caring society.

Since the early 1970s, the constituency of those made dependent on medical and welfare services has begun to move from this position of resignation and passivity to a radicalism based on an understanding of the processes of oppression. Sometimes, people have been regarded as ungrateful, or bitter, or unable to come to terms with their bodily problems, as my colleague Pam Carter wrote, during her period as a cancer survivor:

'I have little difficulty in understanding why the voices of disabled women and others often sound so angry and "difficult". It is terrible to feel real anger, especially when the cause is unjust treatment which is unlikely to be put right. So part of being the helped and not the helper is to be flooded with this kind of anger over and over again. Of course, the cancer literature deals with anger. It is one of the stages of grief, and so on. But it is psychologised and individualised, not analysed in terms of the social relations that it involves. It is the fact that these relations are of inequality that creates the anger, not only the emotional effects of the illness.'

When the helpless become angry, then perhaps it is a sign that things are going to change in the world of welfare. Crucial to this change is the establishment of a sense of self and agency in the face of exclusion and generality. The construction of the Other through the discourses of care and dependency effaces the particularity of Otherness. There is a need for disabled people and Other help-recipients to establish themselves as subjects, each with a voice and rights which are rich enough to respect their individuality while recognising them as a member of the community.

Chapter 2
HELPERS

At first sight, the imagery surrounding helpers in our society seems predominantly positive, focusing on ideas about altruistic sacrifice and beneficent professionalism. For example, doctors are traditionally seen as omnipotent figures, with life-saving powers. The white coat signifies the hygienic, omniscient nature of science, but with overtones of religious power and purification. The stethoscope symbolises the practionerís ability to uncover the truth of the body, and to gain knowledge unavailable to the patient. In television dramas, doctors tend to be successful, authoritative and good, for example Bill Cosbyís character of Dr Huxtable. Nurses, while overlaid with a sexist element of erotic frisson, have an image as angelic helpers, underpaid but devoted to their calling. Again, in the film *Truly, Madly, Deeply*, the heroine, played by Juliet Stevenson, is made a teacher of people with learning difficulties, in order to symbolise her all-round niceness. Workers in the caring professions, with the general exception of social workers, are usually highly valued and respected. Volunteers are seen as pillars of the community, rewarded with medals and admiration. Patients and service users remain silenced, objectified and othered, in a discourse where they exist only to have things done to them or for them.

Looking more closely at images of the doctor in literary works, it is possible to develop a more complex picture, showing the competing representations of the professional helper. The dominant model remains that of the beneficent and altruistic healer. For example, in *Bleak House*, Allan Woodcourt is seldom centre-stage, but is nevertheless held up as an ideal of the medical professional. In his work in the colonies and at home he is self-sacrificing, skilled and motivated by an essential goodness. Esther Summerson – admittedly biased, being his wife – summarises this image of the devoted doctor:

> '*I never walk out with my husband, but I hear the people bless him. I never go into a house of any degree, but I hear his praises, or see them in grateful eyes. I never lie down at night, but I know that in the course of that day he has alleviated pain, and soothed some fellow-creature in the time of need. I know that from the beds of those who were past recovery, thanks have often, often gone up, in the last hour, for his patient ministration.*'
> (Dickens, 1994, 807)

Alternatively, there is the figure of Dr Bovary, in Flaubertís novel *Madame Bovary* (1981). The whole of this novel is a symbolic exploration of normality and deviance, as Flaubert uses the dissatisfaction of Emma Bovary with mundane provincial life to express his own hatred for bourgeois existence. One particular episode explores the role of the professional and the disabled body, when Emma's husband, Charles Bovary, is incited by her and by the chemist Homais to attempt a pioneering operation on the stable-boy, Hippolyte. Hippolyte has a club foot, but is clearly very well adapted to his physical difference. Yet his appearance seems bestial – his foot is 'equine' – and his name reinforces the connection to horses. According to 'progressive' opinion, he must be corrected, brought to conform to the norm. Charles performs this operation, which goes badly wrong, and in the end an older, more traditional doctor has to be summoned to remedy the situation. Dr Bovary highlights the image of the doctor as arrogant, as more concerned with their own fame and success than the well-being of the patient. The doctor knows what is best for the patient, whose role is to provide an opportunity for the demonstration of their power. Moroever the example suggests that doctoring may have dangerous side-effects and unintended outcomes, a process which Ivan Illich has called iatrogenesis. Finally, the episode predicts a world in which medical interventions are normalising, being more concerned with eliminating difference than improving quality of life.

A third literary example highlights the underlying theme of many representations: in Stevenson's *Treasure Island*, Dr Livesey is seen as a gentleman, a person of social power. As a medical practitioner, he is prepared to assist the buccaneers in the enemy camp, but otherwise he is firmly of the Squire's party. Whereas Dr Woodcourt achieves a nobility through his goodness, and Dr Bovary aspires to status through innovative interventions, Dr Livesey reinforces the idea that doctors are commanding figures in society, coming from the upper classes and demanding respect and obedience. That is to say, alongside the image of the doctor as the helper is an equally powerful image of the doctor as someone – usually a man – of authority. The positive image of helpers, therefore, needs to be supplemented by a scepticism as to the role of professionalism. Important questions are raised about the nature of power, the normalising effects of therapy, and the differences in status between helpers and those they aim to serve.

In reality of course, doctors and other professionals are no more consistently altruistic and benign than other human beings. Their ranks include murderers like Dr Crippen, and agents of genocide such as the Nazi doctors or Dr Radovan Karadjic. Alternatively, doctors can be corrupt, inefficient or incompetent, rather than evil, as the Bristol cardiac scandal or the example of consultant gynaecologist Rodney Ledward demonstrates. Yet images of medical and other professionals still tend to be saintly, and systems of accountability and control continue to be inadequate. We should not be surprised by the occasional bad apple, but we should be concerned that so many of them get away with their errors or crimes for so long. The argument of this chapter is that professionalism causes more problems than it solves, and that the power and status of helpers undermine their capacity to help.

One of the major findings of Mildred Blaxter's research into the meaning of disability was the vast complexity of organisations and services which were available to disabled people: her book contains a table of the different sources and types of help which resembles an intricate electronic circuit diagram (Blaxter, 1980, 19). Mike Oliver (1987) quotes a list of the 'helpers' working in the field of disability which includes 23 different categories of professionals, some of them further subdivided. Despite reforms in the NHS and social services, this nightmare of specialisation remains a problem for all those requiring help, whether on the basis of age, disability or other issues. Together with the daunting complexity of welfare benefits, this situation shows exactly how help can be provided in confusing and disempowering ways.

But the scepticism expressed by service users does not concern only the professional maze, but also the role of professionals and the power of professionals. For example, Ken Davis complains about the way that this army of disability professionals refer to people like him as a 'client'. For him, the term 'client' implies a measure of choice – just as when one goes to a solicitor or accountant. Yet disabled people do not have the power to take their custom elsewhere if they are dissatisfied with a disability professional: '*To all intents and purposes, these denizens of the disability industry are the gatekeepers to the services we need. We either go through them or do without. Take it or leave it.*' (Davis, 1993, 197). Davis is sceptical about the role of these professionals, the way they build their careers on the backs of disabled people, and the control they exert over the disabled population, dominating the terminology and philosophy and practices of the 'disability industry'.

Mike Oliver has developed this concept of the disability industry, in order to argue that the real purpose of the welfare state is to benefit those involved in the production of services rather than those involved in their consumption. By far the biggest part of the budget goes on salaries: '*Hence able-bodied professionals consume the employment services of the welfare state to a far greater extent than disabled people consume the health or social services of the very same welfare state.*' (Oliver, 1991, 157). An example he provides is the 1970 Chronically Sick and Disabled Persons Act, which spawned more professionals in social work, occupational therapy and so forth, and became known as 'the professionals' charter'. He refers also to the 1981 Education Act, which raised hopes that disabled children would be integrated into mainstream schools, but, Oliver concludes: *'In fact it resulted in local authorities employing more educational psychologists and administrators in order to keep disabled children in precisely the same places that they were in before the Act was passed.'* (1991, 157).

Millions of people are employed in the health and welfare industries: the National Health Service is the largest employer in the UK. Vic Finkelstein explores the irony that those he calls 'people with abilities' are dependent on disabled people for their salaries and their career development: there is a never-ending demand for more and more health and welfare professionals to *care* for disabled people while the latter remain unemployed or regarded as unemployable.

There is often a significant different in socio-economic status between professionals and those they help, as well as gender and racial differences. Moreover, very few professionals have impairments. For example, the vast majority of doctors are fit and healthy people from higher social classes, who may not be able to understand or relate to the experience of many of their patients. The disabled academic Irving Zola had no illusions about the structural position of doctors in America: *'society is left with the uncomfortable phenomen of a portion of its population, living and living well, off the sufferings of others and to some extent even unwittingly having a vested interest in the continung existence of such problems.'* (1977, 66).

These questions about the parasitic nature of those who are well-paid to provide for those who need help are paralleled by the evidence of the power and status of professionals. Titmuss wrote that professionals are preeminently people with status problems (1968, 72), while for Freidson (1970), the label 'professional' referred to the way in which a group of workers have managed to exert occupational control. Analysts such as Freidson, Zola and Illich have challenged the ideology that professionalism exists to serve patients and service users, and demonstrated the ways in which professionalism can be seen, in reality, to exist to benefit professionals themselves. Making the power of professionals explicit challenges the concept of caring which is the heart of professionalism, creating a dissonance which it is hard to ignore.

In the last decades of the twentieth century, new paradigms of welfare have to a certain extent displaced the power of professionals. Introducing private sector methods into public sector services, in the form of internal markets and managerialism, has undermined the autonomy of professionals – to a large extent in the case of social workers (Harris, 1998), and to a lesser extent in the case of doctors. However, the experience of service users has not been explicitly considered in these changes, even though Conservative governments promoted reform on the basis of consumer choice and power. My contention is that while the working conditions of professionals may have changed, the experience of users has not improved, and that the 'public servants' retain their colonial power. This chapter focuses on doctors, as the ideal-type professional, with shorter discussions of other professionals who aspire to follow the same trajectory of status and control. Finally, there will be a consideration of those helpers who do not enjoy professional status, but may still exert power over those they 'look after'.

Power of definition

A key element in the power of professionals lies in the ability to define the nature of the problem with which they are concerned. This starts with the identification of a need, which justifies the presence and power of the helper:

'Need, used as a noun, became the fodder on which professionals were fattened into dominance.' (Illich, 1977a, 22)

The need has to be translated into a deficiency, meaning something which has to be corrected or compensated for. This deficiency is individualised: the person is taken out of the context which may be the cause of their problem, and structural solutions are ignored for personal ones. For example, corrective surgery – such as cosmetic surgery for people with Downs, or limb-lengthening for people with achondroplasia – is provided instead of working to change the cultural prejudice which makes life difficult for people who look different.

But this definitional power concerns not just the problem itself, but also the person with the problem. The client is constructed by inference through professional definition of need: the disabled person, or the person with mental illness, could be seen as a product of the medical professionals or welfare agencies with which they come into contact. If the individual is the problem, then the professional is the solution. And, because it is in the nature of professions to be self-regulating, it is the professionals themselves who decide whether the help they provide is effective. A combination of medical imperialism, and the tendency of modern societies to give doctors the onus for difficult decisions, ever extends the domain of medicalisation. In Illich's vision of medical nemesis, biomedicine extends its jurisdiction over more and more areas, prescribing drugs to healthy people, undermining the ability of society to look after itself and to experience the natural processes of embodiment, frailty, suffering and death.

Connected with the power of definition is the power of surveillance and identification. Social workers and health visitors enter the home in order to provide advice and counselling, and to inspect childcare standards. Parents are regarded as in need of professional support, as incompetent and deskilled. For Nick Fox, the new professionalisation of care constitutes a technology of surveillance: *'These discourses of care professions create the disciplinary vigil of care, which is more to do with power and control than with values of love, trust and giving.'* (1995, 108). In this analysis, professions are playing a moral role, filling the gap vacated by priests in secular society: *'Professionals tell you what you need, and claim the power to proscribe. They not only recommend what is good, but actually ordain what is right.'* (Illich, 1977a, 17).

By monopolising expertise and extending their power of control, Illich argues that *'the professional has mutated into a crusading and commandeering philanthropist'* (Illich, 1977a, 19). When an elite group of practitioners claim to know best what is right for the public, when there are few democratic controls, it is unsurprising that critics come to believe that professionals are a conspiracy against the people. Lawyers may be the professionals that the public love to hate, but perhaps doctors are the professionals that the public hate to need.

Role of knowledge
The power of definition and surveillance is inextricably entwined with the successful claim to knowledge which lies at the heart of professionalism. By establishing an area of expertise, and excluding others from it, superior status is ensured: the historic process whereby predominantly male obstetricians achieved dominance over female midwives, partly due to monopoly of new techniques such as the forceps, is a classic example of this. Fox's Foucauldian analysis links this superior claim to knowledge with increasing authority over the patient:

> *'The association of power with knowledge suggests that in the context of care, the professionalisation of caring (creating a discipline) cannot but lead to a disciplining of one's clients.'* (Fox, 1995, 111)

Professional codification leads to a body of knowledge which creates a discipline which generates authority and power and enables the professionals to construct the now docile bodies of care recipients. Moreover, as care becomes grounded in scientific knowledge and professional expertise, the patient themselves disappears from the frame. Jewson has written how a reliance on the testimony of the sick person was replaced with an increasing focus on signs and symptoms, the extension of the medical gaze into the body, and the development of diagnostic and now genetic tests. Fox suggests that the result is an edifice of theory and professional discourse which no longer refers explicitly to nursing patients (1995, 114). In our research with disabled children, we often encountered psychologists and other educational professionals who saw the children as diagnostic labels, rather than as people.

The historical trajectory of the medical profession has established a precedent which is now being emulated by lower status professions such as nurses, occupational therapists, and social workers. There is a upward spiral of occupational development by which these related disciplines attempt to monopolise areas of expertise, exclude unqualified practioners from using their job title, and increase their own independence, scope of competence, and hence authority and income. As an example, social work and nursing are both now offered as degree courses, stressing the need for a body of academic knowledge, rather than the vocational training and personal experience which were the former qualifications. This increasing professionalisation of different forms of healing mean that they become ways of exercising power instead of offering service.

According to the Brazilian educationalist Paolo Freire, possession of a body of expertise leads to a proselytising tendency among professionals:

> *'Whatever the speciality that brings them into contact with the people, they are almost unshakeably convinced that it is their mission to 'give' the latter their knowledge and techniques. They see themselves as 'promoters' of the people.'* (1972, 124).

Perhaps this observation takes us back to Dr Bovary, and his orthopaedic experiments. It might also relate to those advocates of eugenics and sexual hygiene in the early twentieth century who campaigned against the unrestrained sexuality of the lower classes, or implemented sterilisation and euthenasia against the hereditarily unfit.

In the modern world, there is therefore an ambivalence in our relationship with doctors. Strident criticisms coexist with deep dependency. For example, within the AIDS field, there is a contradictory relationship with science, in which medics are both allies and enemies. People with the virus do not want their lives to be medicalised, but also do not want to miss out on possible treatments:

> *'Community activists often seem to adopt positions where they are very critical of the claims of bio-medical knowledge while seeking out every "advance" of medical research with an almost religious faith in its findings.'* (Altman, 1994, 121)

Equally, many disabled people survive only because of the effectiveness of modern medicine. Spinal-injured soldiers during the First World War would generally have died very rapidly; during the Second World War, the life expectancy of a spinally injured soldier was about two years; since Vietnam, spinal chord injury no longer implies a significantly shortened lifespan. Another example is the way in which premature babies or people with spina bifida or other congenital impairment are enabled to survive these traumas and grow to adulthood only because of the effectiveness of hospital medicine. Finally, modern pharmaceuticals have ensured that cognitive impairments such as epilepsy and schizophrenia can be managed fairly successfully. Yet disabled people and mental health survivors, alongside people with HIV/AIDS, continue to be strongly critical of the power and role of the medical profession, and with good cause.

There is a paradox here. When we are ill, we want our doctors to be omnipotent. We wish to be able to surrender responsibility and trust them to make us better. It is in our interests to maintain the illusion of the beneficent and all-powerful medical professional, because the alternative is to accept the frightening unpredictability and uncontrollability of human embodiment. We can't live with them, and we can't live without them. Yet, of course, medicine cannot deliver all that it promises, or fulfil all of our hopes. Often doctors promote the idea of their own omniscience, because it suits them and their patients like it. But the reality is that biomedicine cannot solve all the problems, and even causes as many as it solves, for example, through the side-effects of the powerful protease inhibitors taken by people with AIDS, or the increasing problem of drug-resistant bacteria and viruses.

One person with HIV/AIDS whom I interviewed commented about his physicians, *'they don't really have all the answers, do they? They just look at you.'* His monthly visits to the clinic involve an examination of his lungs, eyes and skin, and tests for viral load, liver functions and so forth: his consultations centred on a computer printout. The doctor reassures him that everything is okay, that the clinical signs are all normal. But, as he said to me: *'well it's not – I've got headaches and I've got aching joints.'* In response to this subjective account, the doctor replies to him: *'Don't tell us what's wrong with you. We just want to know about the good things.'* The negative comments are not recorded, only the positive data.

In the disability arts world, there is a joke circulating about doctors which makes a useful comparison. A disabled person dies and goes to Heaven. When

St Peter meets him at the Pearly Gates, he will only enter once he has been assured that there are no doctors in Heaven. Having been ordered around by doctors all his life, he doesn't want to spend eternity dodging members of the medical profession. To his alarm, a few days later he sees a man in a white coat, with a long white beard and a stethoscope round his neck, pushing his way through the crowds of the Blessed. The man in the white coat keeps on repeating *'Get out of my way, I'm a doctor!'*. In horror, the disabled person returns to St Peter and complains about what he has witnessed. St Peter tells him not to be alarmed. *'That's only God. He just thinks he's a doctor.'* Believing in doctors is a bit like believing in God. It is about taking refuge in the hands of one more capable than oneself, who can take responsibility and look after you when things go wrong. Yet doctors are not all-powerful. They cannot live up to the expectation we have of them, because even at best they are fallible, and their remedies have limited efficacy. Perhaps a more balanced appraisal of the success of biomedicine would contribute to a more egalitarian relationship with doctors. Certainly, the present equation of knowledge and power contributes to the alienation of the patient.

Failure of communication
Knowledge also plays a major role in the common complaint that professionals are incapable of communicating properly with patients and service users:

> *'How many leave hospital healed of their physical illness but hurt in their feelings by the impersonal treatment they received; how many return from their consultations with psychiatrists, psychologists, social workers or counsellors, increasingly irritated by the non-committal attitude and professional distance they encounter?'* (Nouwen, 1976, 86)

The origins of this problem may lie in three factors: the inevitable gap between lay and expert knowledge; the way in which doctors are trained and socialised; and the levels of stress involved in practising medicine. The same factors may apply, in different forms, for other professional helpers.

The discursive gap between medical experts and the general public remains, despite the popularity of hospital soap operas. One outcome of the development of medical knowledge may be an increasing distance from lay understanding. This may be a result of the use of incomprehensible jargon or specialist vocabulary: *'The language of modernized professional services mystifies both problem and solution so that citizen evaluation becomes impossible.'* (McKnight, 1977, 86). Because professionals operate in a separate world from the public, and because of the distance that exists between the helper and the helped, serious communication failures can result. As Hugman argues, *'thinking, doing, and speaking the profession cannot be separated'* (Hugman, 1991, 127).

Moreover, the high knowledge requirements of contemporary biomedicine structure the form of the profession. Medical students are selected on the basis of academic success, not skill in communicating or in helping others. Most are white and upper-middle-class, and come from medical families. Many choose medicine because of its material rewards rather than for altruistic reasons. Recruits then go through an intense period of education, which forms a socialisation process which ensures that the new cohort of doctors shares the values of previous generations. Clinical and technical knowledge is prioritised over the learning of communication skills or psychological insight or social understanding, despite recent reforms. Doctors I interviewed felt that their training had been about limiting the imagination, reducing receptiveness and sensitivity, and channelling reading and thinking into narrow paths. For the two to three years of clinical training, the immense pressure of learning and long hours on duty, plus a tendency to socialise almost exclusively with other medics, meant that their cohort of trainees became somewhat removed from the outside world, and abandoned many outside connections and interests. The result was sometimes an 'us and them' mentality, and often a failure to empathise with or understand patients.

Specialisation and experience does not necessarily increase the skills of doctors at dealing with patients. For example, research found that medical students at the beginning of their training were better at engaging with people with profound learning difficulties than those at the end of training (Fraser, 1992, 27). When the public have contact with people with learning difficulties, their attitudes improve, yet research found that trained psychologists had more negative opinions of people with learning difficulties even than unacquainted members of the general public (St Claire, 1986). Again, one doctor I interviewed mentioned a ward round where her consultant, on meeting an older female patient, asked 'How are your thrombi?'. Unsurprisingly, the patient was mystified, at which point the doctor asked, in patronising tones, 'How are your thrombo-embolic phenomena?' It was only after a nurse explained 'He means clots in your legs' that the woman was able to understand and provide the information requested. Clearly the consultant had forgotten that the patient did not have access to professional knowledge, let alone hospital slang.

In fact, the traditional ward round was the key site of failed doctor/patient interaction. Often, consultants still sweep onto wards and into clinics like minor potentates, peremptory, sometimes benign, eternally all-powerful, and arrive at the bedside with an entourage of junior doctors, medical students and nurses. Patients exist to display symptoms, rather than as individuals. Another specialist registrar told me an anecdote about a consultant who said to her: 'I find the ward round goes a lot quicker if you don't talk to the patients.' The ward round has historically existed for the convenience of senior doctors, not the comfort and consolation of patients. It may be an effective means for gathering information, but it is not a private or sensitive context in which to convey serious news. My colleague Pam Carter reflected on the moment she learned of her terminal diagnosis:

> *'I might have been expected to feel ambivalence about doctors. They are the messengers. The knowledge (or often absence of it), power and superior position in every kind of hierachy mean that the possibilities of equality and conversation are slender . . . I have now added to my experience that scene we all know when the consultant delivers his verdict (in my case truly dreadful and no holds barred) not only to me, my partner, his entourage (a large number of whom I had never seen before, as I had not, in fact, seen him), but also I presume to every patient within earshot.'*

Equally distressing anecdotes about the communication of information have been provided by parents of newborn babies with impairments or other complications. SCOPE's Right from the Start campaign challenges the way that professionals break the news of impairment to parents: up to 80 per cent of parents in their survey were dissatisfied with the way professionals had broken the news of their child's disability and with the help given afterwards. The Downs Syndrome Association (Rutter and Seyman, 1999) have collected many examples of the crass and insensitive behaviour of doctors. One mother wrote: '*[The paediatrician] then came back with her, plonked her on my tummy and said, "You have a Mongol".'*. Other parents had been told it would have been better if their baby had died at birth, or asked why they hadn't used amniocentesis. Another mother said: '*We were very badly treated when he was born. We were told he was a rag doll and would be good for nothing.*' No wonder one parent concluded: '*The treatment, understanding and care we received when our son was born was disgusting. I will never forget or forgive the nightmare we had in hospital.*'

The use of the word 'Mongol' in the earlier quotation demonstrates how language can reveal prejudice, as well as creating distance through jargon. Another example is the now declining tendency of doctors to write coded 'diagnoses' on the medical notes of patients, including acronyms such as NON (normal for Newcastle), GOK (God only knows) and SIG (stroppy ignorant git).

Other ways in which communication barriers operate include the tendency to use infantilising terminology – for example in the antenatal encounter – or for professionals to hide behind titles, relying on the anonymity of their role. Sometimes, for instance, a doctor or social worker will be referred to by their surname, while the client is known by their first name.

Many people experience doctors, especially consultants, as arrogant and uncaring. There are perhaps several reasons for this. As observed earlier, doctors tend to be drawn from a narrow stratum at the top of society, and consequently to enjoy the associated confidence, cultural capital and social privileges. Second, Celia Davies argues that the profession is a classic expression of masculinity (1998, 133). The dominant values are impartiality and impersonality: control of emotion, detachment, autonomy. Senior doctors depend on the adjunct work of others to prepare and clean up after them, usually female nurses, technicians and orderlies. They are used to being obeyed, facilitated, supported, respected, all of which contributes to egotism. Moreover the male culture means that women, to get ahead, have to emulate the men and suppress elements of empathy or softness which might be associated with femininity

Moreover, unlike the traditional image of God, or of the loving parent, with the best will in the world, doctors do not see our ailments in the way we do. For us, our problem is the centre of our life. Whether it is a nagging pain, or a chronic illness, or a worry about the implications of a lump or a sensation, it is of literally life-and-death importance to us. The doctor's diagnosis, and the doctor's treatment, cannot be more vital. Yet, for the doctor, we are just one of a number of patients they are seeing that day, one of hundreds of thousands they will see over their career. Our cancer or our back pain is just another example of a condition with which they are tediously familiar, and they cannot be expected to see it in the way we do.

Therefore perhaps it is wrong to see the doctor as cruel or uncaring. It is just that he or she cannot be expected to empathise, both because they do not know what it is like and because they know just what it is like. This is why medical information may sometimes be communicated with a lack of sensitivity. For the professional it may be routine and insignificant. For the individual it is devastating, unrepeatable and profound. The whole universe is contained in that moment, whereas for a doctor it is a difficult or sad or tiresome task during a long and stressful day or week. Again, many doctors may not be emotionally or psychologically equipped for the stress of communicating terrible diagnoses, which may lead to what seems like abruptness.

Finally, the nature of medical practice perhaps demands a certain level of arrogance and detachment. The responsibility of performing a major operation, or presiding over a birth, could be difficult to take on unless one is supremely confident in one's own abilities. Cutting off from any idea that the body before you is a real person, whose life is literally in your hands, may be necessary before making an incision into their flesh. Equally, if one is to endure the suffering and death of others on a daily basis, perhaps a psychic defence is to distance oneself, not just from people on an individual basis, but also from patients as a class of person. Recognising one's own frailty and mortality in every person one treats may be an impossible barrier to continuing practice. Of course, there are many kinds of doctor. The personalities, and reputations, of surgeons and gynaecologists are different from those of general practitioners and psychiatrists, both because different people enter those specialisms, and also because there are distinct strains and pressures, and different relationships with patients. Yet medicine remains perhaps the profession with the most weighty responsibilities, and the National Health Service one of the most stressful sectors in which to work.

Low status helpers

Many of the issues which are exemplified in the case of doctors are also evidenced in the practice of social workers and others working in the social welfare field. However, the levels of autonomy and power decrease further down the occupational ladder, particularly as the tasks carried out by social workers and care assistants, for example, are not technically complex or highly specialised. Nurses, social workers and care assistants work within bureaucratic structures which place limits on their role and the way in which help can be delivered. Like doctors, these lower-status helpers work within a tradition which explains social problems such as disability in individualistic terms.

Both social workers and nurses have their origins in nineteenth-century philanthropy. In their origins, these occupations are associated with the idea of vocation and service to others – taking the form of the devotion and selflessness which was of course particularly associated with women. Nurses were taught to be silent in the face of rudeness, insults and general lack of respect from some doctors. Lack of power, poor pay and conditions, and the competing demands of professionals on the one hand, and patients and users on the other, mean that the role of social worker, nurse and care assistant can be experienced as thankless and stressful. Such workers face all the difficulties of working as a helper, without the status and other privileges enjoyed by doctors and other higher professionals. Bombarded with work, the result can be a failure to deliver effective helping:

'*Their senses become dulled and their sensibilities blunted; they suffer from emotional saturation or drought. Their helping can become automatic, unspontaneous and quite joyless – they come to resent their clients.*' (Jordan, 1979, 29). Jordan suggests that occupational hazards of these roles include insecurity, pressure, defensiveness, anxiety and lack of confidence.

Care assistants, perhaps entirely lacking in training or qualifications, are among the lowest-paid and most exploited members of the workforce. As Colin Barnes (1990) observed in his study of day centres, they may have much in common with the disabled people whom they are paid to support. The consequence of the exploitation of the workforce may be depersonalisation of the clients, as in old people's homes:

'*Depersonalizing the people being cared for, disaggregating them into a series of tasks is a way whereby staff can protect themselves from confronting the pain of people-processing organizations where both carers and cared-for alike are devalued by and unsupported in their social context.*' (Fennell et al., 1988, 144)

Kathryn Ellis (1993) attributes some of the low morale expressed by social workers to their new role as gatekeepers within community care, working within a financially constrained environment: they have a problem of dual accountability, to the agency for which they work, and to the user whom they are professionally bound to support and help. She proposes a more explicit set of rationing criteria, so that decisions can be understood or challenged.

Disabled people and other service users express many criticisms of the resulting attitude and performance of low-status helpers. Some comments relate to the bureaucratic context in which helpers work, the maze of regulations and the lack of flexibility. For example, district nurses are restricted to nursing tasks, delivering a service which fails to assist disabled people to exert control over their lives. Whereas home helps started out as cleaners, since the advent of comunity care they have replaced social workers as cheaper, lower-status, care workers. Home helps also take over from nurses, taking on roles such as changing dressings. Although home helps may be cheaper, they lack proper training. And the result is that homecare no longer provides the housework and shopping which was traditionally the task of the home help

Other complaints relate to the way services are delivered. For example, people do not like the way their homes are invaded by strangers and the resulting lack of privacy. There may be a lack of continuity of care because a different helper arrives each week. Helpers may be late or unreliable. For example, service users report that uncertainty over what time the nurse will arrive to help with a bath can disrupt half a day and cause stress. Helpers may ignore the disabled or elderly person and talk to an able-bodied relative or carer instead, or may be patronising or bossy. Gay disabled people have sometimes complained about the homophobia of home helps or care assistants. Helpers cause problems when they move things around the house, causing unseen hazards for blind people, or making it difficult to find things. Their help may be experienced as meddling and interference, rather than responsive assistance.

There is a considerable level of antagonism and cynicism towards the social work profession from disabled people and their organisations, as my 1996 research with disabled people revealed. One activist said to me: '*I am appalled at the standard of qualified social workers.*' Respondents '*struggled to see a role for social workers in disability*', because it was felt that social workers had nothing useful to offer disabled people, not being skilled in equipment, design, planning or welfare rights: '*in disability, social work is a redundant profession*'. There was scepticism regarding the skills and appropriateness of social workers fulfilling a counselling role. Neither was multi agency working or the multidisciplinary culture felt to be a reality: '*the culture isn't there for them to be effective coordinators or assessors*'.

Social workers are now mainly involved in care management, rather than direct help, yet they are still often resented by disabled people. Many service users feel unhappy because of lack of knowledge of their entitlements. In a context of financial constraint, it is cheaper not to give full information of what might be available: in this way, ignorance is a form of rationing because, as one person said, '*What you don't know, you don't get.*' Regulations provide further barriers: for example, one man I interviewed had been told that he would not qualify for an electric wheelchair if he was able to walk around inside the house. Yet, for him, the point of the wheelchair was to get out and travel around the neighbourhood, which he could not manage. Again, although hc had received a manual wheelchair, no one was able to help when it needed to be mended. Such experiences seem to provide more evidence for the suggestion that the current situation is one of minimal services, maximum dependency.

However, there are signs of different models developing, bypassing the situation of statutory social workers trapped between the pressures of community care procedures and the frustration and antagonism of disempowered disabled clients. Often this is in voluntary organisations, and particularly through self-organised voluntary groups such as the Spinal Injuries Association (d'Aboville, 1991). In these examples, social workers are not operating as gatekeepers to state benefits and services, and workers and clients are able to interact in a situation of respect and mutual equality, without the barriers of professional expertise or statutory restriction.

Training for social workers, home helps and care assistants is vitally important. Disability equality issues, for example, need to be central to the course, rather than the traditional medical and psychosocial models of intervention. Collective and structural issues, rather than an individual approach, must be prioritised. Yet my research into social work education suggests that the dominant philosophy of social work education, often based on trying to under-stand '*what it's like*' for clients, does not sit well with the principles of disability equality. The medical model assumption that impairment is inevitably bad predominates in thinking. Anti-discriminatory practice is often an adjunct to professional and practice issues rather than a substantive core of it. However, evidence shows that it is possible to develop social-model approaches to social work and disability (Morris, 1994a, 23ff.) This also means drawing on new ways of working, stressing partnership and mutuality, and adapting training to the changing roles of social workers.

Changing professions
In the 1980s and 1990s, new health and welfare approaches have challenged the dominance of professionals such as doctors and social workers, while not necessarily increasing accountability to service users, or improving the face-to-face relationship. The Conservative government introduction of market principles into medical and social services were ostensibly designed to increase efficiency and consumer choice, although the changes seem in retrospect to have been about the commodification and rationing of the welfare state.

One key dimension of the change was the increase in managerialism. For example, social workers' roles have changed from direct casework towards the assessment and management of care packages. In general there has been an attempt to circumscribe the power of professionals through managerialism and restructuring. This is partly a response to various social services scandals and attacks on social work by the media and the right. Private sector emphases on flexibility, innovation, quality control and auditing now dominate public services. It is an open question as to whether it is better to be on the receiving end of the new rationalised management structures or the traditional relation-ship-based social work practice with all the difficulties which disabled radicals have identified. Neither is adequate or ideal.

In particular, the new processes of needs assessment cannot accommodate individuated recognition and mutual response:

'Any sense of the richness and incommensurability of human need has been lost because its grounding in specific human histories and relationships cannot be interrogated in standardised assessment formats, and the meeting of such needs poses awesome problems of auditing.' (Froggett, 1996, 119)

Not all service users will need the psychosocial aspect of help, but the new system may leave those service users who do missing out on a vital element of the social work role unless these needs can be met in a different way. Perhaps there it is important to ensure that social work practice involves a relationship with users, as well as the procedural rights-based approach. David Howe develops a powerful argument for the return of psychodynamically informed practice, to improve client's security, self-esteem, self-efficacy and sense of autonomy, rather than attempting *'to deal with human distress and difficulty by use of impersonal statutes and rote-responses'* (Howe, 1998, 54).

Another element of the new service discourse was a stress on consumerism. While left critics of welfare services had campaigned for welfare rights and against paternalism, the new stress on service users as customers was based on the model of the market, the extension of choice, and an attack on 'the collectivist state' (Crinson, 1998, 230). For example, John Major's government introduced the Patient's Charter, which gave token 'rights' to health service users. Again, publishing league tables of hospitals provides the illusion of patient choice, in a context of continuing cash constraints on the National Health Service and increasingly interventionist management from central government. There has been limited empowerment for service users, despite the talk of partnership. While New Labour have reduced the role of the market, they remain committed to the concept of the Patient's Charter, and to the consumerist rhetoric of choice, rather than the radical concept of democratic accountability and community participation.

Finally, as a reaction to notorious bad cases, the late 1990s have seen another attempt to place medical practice under lay scrutiny. The advent of clinical governance suggests that the traditional autonomy of the doctor will be eroded further. Tory reforms exerted organisational and budgetary control over practitioners, and were consequently resisted by professional groupings. The Commission for Health Improvement, and moves towards revalidation, should ensure that doctors are held to account for their skills, and are an advance over the self-policing of the General Medical Council. Now social and communication skills should be stressed alongside technical competence, and training should highlight the art of medicine alongside the science. It remains to be seen whether these innovations will genuinely improve services to patients, or merely add stress and anxiety to doctors' lives without weeding out the minority of incompetent practitioners.

No-status helpers

At the bottom of the helping hierachy come the unpaid, non-status carers and volunteers who provide services out of love and duty. Many commentators have demonstrated how the current framework of community care places the responsibility for supporting disabled and elderly people predominantly on unpaid carers. The welfare state is saved the cost of professional help in the home, and also the cost of residential care for those who could not cope independently in the community. There has been considerable concern over the impact on those who provide this help: feminists particularly have challenged the tendency for women to be the major carers. As Gillian Dalley suggests, *'Women have internalised the altruistic ideal; society has capitalised on it'* (1988, 18). More recently, the situation of children caring for disabled parents has also been identified and challenged. People who need help are devalued, and so is the process of providing ordinary and everyday forms of help: *'Caring is often constituted socially in a way that makes caring work into the work of the least well off members of society'* (Tronto, 1993, 112).

In this discussion, however, I will be taking the part of those disabled feminists who have challenged the construction of the caring debate, in order to explore the ways in which those who receive care are disempowered and marginalised. This is not to deny the major and negative impacts on unpaid carers: as Brandon writes about caring in general, *'Helping is not socialized masochism and the helper has also a right to satisfaction, joy and love from the process'* (1990, 27). Instead, it is to express scepticism about the caring industry and concern that the very real problems of those who provide care may distract from and take priority over the rights of those who receive it. For many disabled or older people, relying totally on one person when they are a partner or a parent leads to powerlessness and isolation. In the worst cases, people may suffer neglect or abuse.

Both the contemporary profile and the whole concept of the carer orginated as recently as the 1980s. For example, the Carers National Association was formed in 1986. A key 'moral entrepreneur' in the social construction of the category was Jill Pitkeathley, whose book defined a carer as

> *'someone whose life is in some way restricted by the need to be responsible for the care of someone who is mentally ill, mentally handicapped, physically disabled or whose health is impaired by sickness or old age.'* (1989, 11)

This statement shows how the notion of the carer rests on the construction of the category of helpless person who requires care. The terminology used by Pitkeathley includes words such as 'dependent person', 'sufferers', 'heavily dependent person'. Two key distinctions are suggested: first, 'caring' is reserved for unpaid rather than paid care; second, 'normal' caring (for example, caring for children) is differentiated from this other kind of caring, which is not time-limited or reciprocal. Yet while children eventually grow up, elderly relatives eventually die. And surely you care for your elderly relatives because they cared for you, and your own children may do the same for you in future.

In stressing the problems of carers, Pitkeathley makes totalising generalisations that stress the negative rather than the positive aspects of the relationship, and that reinforce the idea of the helped person as burden. For example, she suggests that carers experience isolation, being undervalued, fear, resentment, anger, guilt, embarrassment, role reversal, sense of loss, effects of emotional stress, strain on relationships and bereavement. Undoubtedly many do, but the effect is to blame the victim, and to ignore the structural causes of the difficulties facing carers.

The solutions proposed by Pitkeathley echo those feminists who proposed institutionalisation and residential care: for example, she talks about the need to move away from a nuclear family model towards a collectivist approach. Yet she does not consider the views and preferences of disabled and older people themselves. Again, she opposes the idea that direct payments to disabled people would solve the problem of unpaid and exploitative care: because of her overwhelming focus on the needs of the carer, she suggests that the money should go direct to them, not to the service users. Much of the philosophy, if not the financial suggestions, contained in Pitkeathley's book went into the 1995 Carers Act, which defined a carer defined as someone providing more than 20 hours of care per week.

For the disability movement, the key to solving the problem of care is to empower disabled people themselves. For example, direct payments would allow disabled people to employ personal assistants rather than rely on unpaid care. Equally, given the contentious academic debates about the role of children as carers, proper personal assistance schemes would avoid this necessity. When I interviewed disabled people about community care in 1996, many voiced suspicion that meeting the needs of carers is seen by government as a cheaper option in the short term. Carers have the 'moral high ground', and are seen as safe. It was suggested that statutory services found it easier to consult and talk with carers than with disabled people, and this could be a way in which consultation bypasses disabled users: the phrase 'users and carers' was a way of avoiding disabled people. One disabled respondent spoke bitterly about his local carers' organisation, which did not even have a fully accessible building: *'I wish I had kinder things to say about carers' organisations. I don't.'* He went on to add, *'to my mind, the more you increase the rights of carers, the more you take them away from disabled people'*.

Disabled commentators recognise the difficulties facing carers, but stress equally the origins of the problem in the oppression of disabled people. As Morris argues, *'Relying on a family member creates significant restraints on the autonomy of both the disabled person and the person providing the help'* (1993, 153). The stress on commonality highlights, for example, that residential care itself involves the exploitation of poorly paid and often female staff; that many carers are men; that the majority of the people receiving care are themselves women; and that many care users are also care providers, for example as parents themselves or as children of ageing parents. This evidence goes some way to dissolving the polarity between carers and cared-for. Drawing on Morris's work, Bill Bytheway and Julia Johnson (1998) have analysed the social construction of 'carers', and challenged the perspective of the carers' movement. They highlight the concept of 'caring systems' in which mutuality plays a key role, and conclude that care should be reconceived as a normal part of ordinary family and community life.

Conclusion

This chapter has stressed the potential and actual conflict between helpers and those with whom they work. Whereas the dominant helper images are benign, the everyday experience of helpers is often dehumanising and unsatisfactory. Organisations of disabled people, people with HIV/AIDS, older people and mental health system survivors have come together in the 1990s, often to challenge the attitudes and practices of mainstream helping systems and to campaign for change. Key to this has been the provision of peer support and mutual aid: rather than relying on professionals or others who do not know what it is like to experience the situation, people learn from and rely on each other for advice and services. By becoming more informed and self-confident, people can demand their rights and better treatment. Moreover, organisations are ways for the voice of users to be heard within statutory and voluntary organisations, and play a role in advocating change in practice. Consumerism was a key element in the Conservative rhetoric of community care, and democratisation is part of the Labour repertoire of values: in practice, openings for consultation and participation have been brief and transitory. User involvement should become a key part of the setting of priorities and the delivery of services.

If organisations of the marginalised can become established, they may provide an effective counterweight for professional dominance. This might be a move towards the accountability of local authorities and of professional groupings. Statutory services are formally accountable through the processes of local democracy, but these can be inaccessible or difficult to affect from outside the system. But consultative procedures and the advocacy of organised user interests may lever change, in the way that, for example, police forces may be held to account through police authorities, community liaison and open meetings. The aim should be to achieve a partnership between helpers and those they help on a collective level, in order that individual encounters are made more humane and egalitarian. For example, self-assessment by people who receive services could replace the 'expert' assessment of professional care-managers.

Professionals are here to stay. André Gorz argues for the removal of status, stratification and hierachy from specialisation:

> *'I have nothing against professionals. They will always be there. There will always be surgeons, for example. The only question is how we stop them forming a class or caste, how we stop them doing nothing but exercise and monopolise their skills, thus turning these into a source of power.'* (Gorz, 1985, 76)

Whatever its problems as a noun, 'professional' remains an adjective to aspire to. It suggests exacting standards of self-judgement, and values such as confidentiality, competence and trust. Perhaps the key to progress is reducing the gap between helper and helped. The origins of the word 'therapy', for instance, lie in the Greek *therapeuein*, meaning 'to accompany, to serve': this implies an empathy and shared endeavour in which helper and helped are open to change. Greater collective organisation and political strength of user constituencies will aid the balancing of power. But professionals will need to relinquish some of their status, and recognise the humanity and vulnerability which they share with the people for whom they work.

Albert Memmi asks what happens to the coloniser who refuses. They operate in a difficult position because they cannot escape from a concrete situation. But those who have historically dominated can contribute to a more equal relationship in future. After all, helpers themselves will inevitably need to be helped one day. Distinctions, such as separate toilets and canteens, should be removed, and with them the manner in which professionals provide help in ways that bolster their own status at the cost of those who are helped. David Brandon suggests that *'We can gain professional confidence and personal security at our consumer's expense – by taking over the running of his life'* (1990, 40). He also quotes a memorable phrase from Tolstoy: *'I sit on a man's back, choking him and making him carry me, and yet assure myself and others that I am very sorry for him and wish to ease his lot by all possible means – except by getting off his back'* (1990, 6).

Removing the distinctions and standing shoulder to shoulder is also about recognising the ways in which everyone – not just professionals – is a helper and a healer. Specialisation means that our everyday capacities and responsibilities for helping ourselves and others are denied, and the role is handed over to the professional doctor or social worker. User groups and mutual aid and support networks are ways in which the helped can themselves become helpers. We should not expect people in formal helping roles to achieve standards which we do not achieve ourselves. The listening which is key to real helping is a capacity which is open to everyone:

> *'Healing is the humble but also very demanding task of creating and offering a friendly empty space where strangers can reflect on their pain and suffering without fear, and find the confidence that makes them look for new ways right in the centre of their confusion.'* (Nouwen, 1976, 90)

Chapter 3
HELPING

Preceding chapters have explored the cultural meaning and social context of receiving and providing help, focusing on the roles and individuals involved on either side of the equation. In this chapter, I will discuss the process of providing help in modern British society, looking at three paradigmatic examples before reflecting on the process of altruism itself.

1. The *family* is the archetypal unit of mutual aid, and is associated with very positive, and often very romanticised, notions of selflessness and support. Yet it is also the concept from which we ultimately derive our notions of patriarchy and paternalism, and writers from the feminist and psychodynamic traditions have challenged the beneficent ideal of domesticity.

2. *Charity* is strongly valued in all religious traditions. It expresses the voluntary response of the community towards those in need, and particularly those who are the casualties of cruel social conditions such as war, famine or *laissez-faire* capitalism. Donating money or time to help the less fortunate remains a social ideal, as the popularity of telethons and aid appeals seems to indicate. Yet, particularly from the disability movement, a powerful critique has developed of the way that the helping impulse has been institutionalised through large quasi-business voluntary organisations.

3. *Welfare state* provision arose from the social democratic and liberal traditions, particularly in the postwar period, to express social responsibility for collective needs such as health, education and those excluded from the labour market. Yet, despite regular processes of reform and renewal, social services in particular have been criticised as unresponsive, undemocratic, and ineffective in fostering independence and social inclusion.

As well as providing relief, both informal and formal helping have promoted dis-welfares by failing to recognise the personal dignities and citizenship rights of those who receive help. The persistent devaluing of care-receivers, explored in the first chapter, is expressed in the lack of a voice, in the lack of choice and autonomy, and in the status gap which helping reinforces. Therefore it may be necessary to suspend the positive values which are associated with helping in our society, and to look more critically at the actually existing relationships of care which we take for granted.

One way to begin the deconstruction is to turn to a symbolic exploration in the artistic field which embodies themes that often emerge from the testimony of people who are made dependent. Two sculptures by Lebanese/British contemporary artist Mona Hatoum illustrate the dilemma at the heart of the helping relationship. *Untitled (Wheelchair)* (1998) is a stainless steel structure resembling a conventional wheelchair. Bare and clinical, and looking very uncomfortable, it is reduced to a simple arrangement of bars and sheets of metal. It has four small wheels, which clearly could not be manipulated by anyone sitting in the chair. Yet the two handles, which would enable someone to push the chair from behind, are formed into sharp carving knives. It would be impossible to take hold of them without being sliced or spiked. The sculpture seems like a modern, medical, rendering of Boadicea's chariot with its wheel blades. What are we to make of this shocking apparatus? Its extraordinary power as an object comes from the collision of caring and cruelty which it represents. Hatoum's *Incommunicado* (1993) has the same effect. The piece is a simple, institutional cot made of bare steel, but instead of a mattress it has a base of rows of thin wire, making it like a person-sized egg slicer. Both these works challenge our understanding of the help that is extended to vulnerable or dependent people, whether babies or adults. The clinical functionality of the equipment suggests that only the bare minimum of help is being offered, without any affection or real warmth. The cot-as-torture apparatus suggests that caring can conceal violence and abuse. The wheelchair-with-knives also suggests to me the powerlessness of the person using the wheelchair, and a sense of resentment at being dependent on someone else to push one around. Enshrined in steel, both the dependency of the user and the hostility towards the helper are a product of the physical arrangement of the chair.

Both artworks are about contradiction. *Untitled (Wheelchair)* denies reciprocity between user and carer, but also offers the contradiction that the chair can neither be propelled by its user, nor pushed by somone else. Partly perhaps this should read as a statement about the contemporary western fixation with independence. In western society, indivudalism and autonomy are of the highest value. People are unable to accept help without losing a sense of self. In societies such as the one from Hatoum originates there is more of a sense of interdependence and reciprocity in which both the community and the family are more important, and perhaps this cultural difference is underlined in the artwork. Yet also, and most disturbingly, the sculptures point to the way in which care and cruelty can be intimately related, and to what Zygmunt Bauman (1993) calls the 'intimate dialectics of love and domination'. Hatoum's work prompts the questions which are posed in this discussion of the helping relationship. What are the motivations of those who help others? How is helping experienced by the others who are helped? What are the psychological and institutional models for helping? It is my argument that helping, in our society, has operated as a form of colonialism. Represented as beneficence, it sometimes operates as oppression.

Family and parenting
The ideology of the family exerts a powerful influence on our understanding of helping, and it casts a long shadow over the contemporary arrangement of community care (Dalley, 1988). As feminists have shown, too much of community care rests ultimately on the unpaid caring work of women in the home, who are expected to be the natural carers of people who are chronically ill or impaired, or who are elderly. Care is seen to belong in the idealised nuclear family, while paid care is viewed as second best. So the emphasis of much social policy is on sustaining family care, and when voluntary agencies or the state provide residential care as an alternative to the family, it tends to reinforce the same model (Brechin *et al.*, 1998). Yet, while family care and the ënormal home' are meant to be the ideal, social research and analysis also suggest we should be suspicious or cautious about what goes on in the domestic environment. Parental love and support, which we have been led to expect as unlimited and unconditional, seems to be more unreliable than ideology claims.

Gay writers have explored the way that parents may reject their homosexual children: many gay people reject the intolerance they experience from their family of birth, and turn instead to create alternative models of family in the form of networks of friends and partners within gay communities. Researchers involved in the 'families of choice' project stress the choice and agency in this new idea of family:

> '*In the family stories being told at the end of the twentieth century there is a sense that, for some, family is something you create for yourself, something that involves interactions, commitments and responsibilities that are negotiated in a world where few things are pre-given or certain.*'
> (Heaphy *et al.*, 1999, 3)

This has been a particular aspect of resistance and survival during the AIDS crisis: friends as well as partners have been providers of care. Kinship has been about choice and self-determination, and the crisis has led to a particular valuing of the institution of friendship, based on mutal help, support, love and trust in a community context.

Feminist writers have explored the dominance of men over women which takes place within the home, and the tendency towards economic and sexual exploitation within heterosexuality (Barrett and McIntosh, 1991). Equally the inequality of parent and child may contribute to emotional or physical disempowerment. The late twentieth-century realisation of the extent of child abuse – physical or sexual – suggests a contradiction between the myth of the family and the reality of some domestic practices. So, too, a growing realisation of the phenomenon of elder abuse makes us cautious about the ways in which not just institutions, but also private houses, conceal cruel or exploitative practices.

At a less extreme level, professions such as health visiting have always occupied a role as agents of surveillance and control over families, and mothers in particular (Donzelot, 1980; Bloor and McIntosh, 1990). Rather than caring being natural or automatic, it is now suggested that parents require tuition in how to be effective parents, not only in terms of exerting moral authority, but also in terms of basic techniques such as bathing babies or providing appropriate diets for infants. Contemporary concerns about uncontrollable youth often contain an element of blame towards parents for failing to exert proper care and control, for example, with the advent of parenting orders.

But we also know that there are many ways in which parents can, at a very ordinary level, undermine the personhood or infringe the basic rights of their children. Many people still believe that it is correct and sensible to hit a child, whereas acts of violence between adults would not be condoned. The growing literature in the new sociology of childhood shows how children are denied independence and autonomy not only in society, but also in the home. Often this may stem from over protection, which originates in the best possible motives. Very commonly, parents of teenagers have difficulty in letting go: in recognising that their children now need to move away and make their own lives. We laugh at the sit-com stereotype of the controlling mother. Yet the humour comes from recognition that this transmutation of love and concern into control and domination is common to many families.

Parents of disabled children, for example, may feel that their children are vulnerable, or incapable of exercising choices, and thus require guidance and direction at all times. Often people with physical impairments and especially learning difficulties are maintained in a protected and childlike dependency long after non-disabled young people have 'grown up'. When parents are needed to provide care to their older disabled children, they may be unable to see them as adults in their own right. Because they provide physical support, they may feel it necessary to provide emotional and social support, and even take decisions for the disabled person. One disabled woman referred to her own experience of relying on her parents for support by saying '*give an inch and they take a mile*'. It is common to find that older parents of people with learning difficulties are keen for them to be institutionalised, for fear of what might happen to them after their own death, despite those who advocate a greater independence for those who are often adult children. Part of this is an understandable fear about the quality of services, and the realisation that respite and residential care fails to meet the needs of disabled people effectively, or to respect the individuality and human rights of service users. But there is also here an extension of the feelings of indispensability which are part of the psychological gains that parents achieve from looking after children. Having power over others may bolster self-esteem and provide satisfaction, and for this reason it may be hard to let go or to recognise the other's need for independence.

The new sociology of childhood has demonstrated that young people are not passive receptors of socialisation, or 'inferior adults', but active agents, able to express feelings about their lives and their wishes: for example, Priscilla Alderson's (1993) work has shown that children are able to make sophisticated judgements about having surgery. Physical immaturity does not translate into social or moral incompetence, despite the ideology of childhood innocence and the need for parental protection. Evidence from psychoanalysis demonstrates the harming outcomes of particular parent–child relationships long into adult life. Effective parenting, like effective helping in other spheres, comprises a balance between direct care and fostering autonomy. It involves recognising the agency and independence of children as separate people. It means hearing the voice of young people, rather than relying on the old adage about children being 'seen and not heard'. It relies on values like trust and respect, as much as the altruism and concern which are the dominant associations of parenting.

The problem is that the traditional myths of parenting as benign and appropriate become transferred outside the home into caring situations, which are often designed to be as much like 'normal families' as possible. Geraldine Lee-Treweek's research in care homes shows how carers can infantilise older people, and treat them as if they are their parents (1996). A subconscious model of the family dominated a set of relationships in which physically capable older people were expected to submit to total surveillance. Lee-Treweek labels the group who conformed to this caring model as 'the lovelies': they would get cuddled, kissed and tucked in, as positive rewards for their compliance. Another group of residents, who resisted the baby-talk and other patronising processes, were labelled 'the disliked', and seen as troublesome and demanding for rejecting the emotional order of the home. The final group were 'the confused', who were pitied, and seen as sweet and cute and comical. My own experience of working in a hospital for people with learning difficulties echoes Lee-Treweek's research: residents tended to be seen either as sweet and innocent and childlike, or as threatening and unpredictable and dangerous. Of course, these values can also be associated with children – either the charming five-year-old, or the challenging teenager – and a parent–child model tended to dominate interactions. In both these examples, emotional work is a way of empowering the workers, and of rationalising a situation which is outside normal expectation. Manipulation of the service users (who, in Lee-Treweek's case, were actually paying for the service) is achieved via a nurturant power that echoes the dominance in many real parenting situations.

It is vital therefore to understand the way that unhelpful helping begins in the home, and is then replicated in the helping promoted by welfare arrangements which seek to duplicate the home. The 'naturalisation' of help should be replaced with a sensitivity to the ways in which help may harm. Consistent respect for the dignity and autonomy of children, disabled people and older people needs urgently to be inserted into conventional approaches to family and non-family care.

Images like those of Mona Hatoum bring to the surface a realisation of the anger and antipathy which may underlie altruism. Another shocking metaphor for power and dependency within the family comes in Kafka's story, *Metamorphosis*. Gregor Samsa, a young clerk, wakes up one morning to find that he has been transformed into a giant beetle. Kafka's work is about the human condition in general, and the problems of bourgeois life in particular, but his story can also be seen as a metaphor for disability. Gregor's metamorphosis parallels the change brought about by a spinal injury, or stroke. At first, he is unable to accept or understand the change in his physicality. Later, he learns to forget his old way of moving around, and to adapt to the best way of standing and walking in his new body. The focus of the story is on how Gregor's parents reject him, and how his family comes to see him as a burden and an embarrassment, and as a disgrace. Metamorphosis echoes the difficulty that families may sometimes have in dealing with unexpected, irreversible change, and their resentment against a disabled family member. It also reminds us that many people are very uncomfortable with disability: it may be a threat, or something to be feared.

Charities

The sentimentalisation of domesticity and the ideology of the patriarchal family were products of the Victorian middle classes. The institution of charity is another manifestation of altruism which took a recognisably modern form in the nineteenth century. It also provides examples of the way in which helping can harm, and of the self-serving nature of seemingly beneficent social arrangements. As industrial capitalism developed, within the *laissez-faire* economics of Victorian England, so the problem arose of how to deal with the excluded, or the orphaned, or the aged or the disabled. Philanthropists on the one hand, and social campaigners on the other, developed organisations and institutions to meet the imperative of help for the casualties of the economic system.

Yet, from the earliest, humanitarians were identifying and criticising the short-comings of charitable provision. The novels of Charles Dickens are full of unforgettable images of charitable institutions such as schools and orphanages, and the cold regimes or exploitative overseers with which they were associated. So, in *Hard Times*, he mercilessly parodies the utilitarian philosophies of the day, in the person of Gradgrind. In *Bleak House*, the grotesque Mrs Jellyby is eternally preoccupied with her activities of 'telescopic philanthropy': for example, she is always writing letters on behalf of her Borioboola Ba charity. As the lawyer Kenge tells Esther, our heroine,

> '*Mrs Jellyby*' . . . *is a lady of very remarkable strength of character, who devotes herself entirely to the public. She has devoted herself to an extensive variety of public subjects, at various times, and is at present (until something else attracts her) devoted to the subject of Africa . . .*'
> (Dickens, 1994, 31)

Meanwhile, the home and family of Mrs Jellyby are entirely neglected. Another do-gooder, Mrs Pardiggle, takes Esther on one of her trips to visit the homes of working-class people. Dickens viciously satirises her patronising do-goodism, and her tendency to blame the individuals for living in squalor, rather than putting their plight into the context of social and economic oppression. He puts a speech of bitter class resentment into the mouth of the bricklayer whose family is the subject of Mrs Pardiggle's charitable endeavours:

> '*I wants it done, and over. I wants a end of these liberties took with my place. I wants a end of being drawed like a badger. Now you're a-going to poll-pry and question according to custom – I know what you're a-going to be up to. Well! You haven't got no occasion to be up to it. I'll save you the trouble . . .*' (Dickens, 1994, 98)

As an analyst of the charity industry concludes,

> *'There is strong evidence that the Victorian poor were not content with their lot. Contemporary reports suggest irritation with the moralising cant of the relief workers, and resentment at providing a hobby for the evangelical middle classes whose women were precluded by custom from gainful employment.'* (Williams, 1989, 44)

Yet Dickens is not arguing against altruism or kindness: when Esther herself intervenes to help the family – as when she later nurses Jo through his smallpox – it is clear that her help is humane and unpatronising and well-motivated.

Dickens's target is the class which presides over an economic system in which people like the bricklayer's family, or the streetsweeper Jo, or Betty Higden in *Our Mutual Friend*, are the ultimate casualties. The latter would rather die in the fields than submit to the indignities of the workhouse:

> *'Old Betty Higden however tired, however footsore, would start up and be driven away by her awakened horror of falling into the hands of Charity. It is a remarkable Christian improvement, to have made a pursuing Fury of the Good Samaritan; but it was so in this case, and it is a type of many, many, many.'* (Dickens, 1985a, 569)

Later Dickens suggests ironically that people like her would doubtless appreciate the Poor Law more philosophically on an income of ten thousand a year. In the moral landscape of *Our Mutual Friend*, we are meant to understand that working-class people – like Betty Higden or Lizzie Hexham herself – may have a nobility and dignity and moral worth far superior to the ladies and gentlemen who gather at the table of the Veneerings. Because the upper classes are oblivious or uncaring about the plight of the poor, the moral responsibility belongs to them. So, when Jo, the lowest of the low, finally dies, Dickens's sentimentalism also has a hard political edge:

> *'Dead, your Majesty. Dead, my lords and gentlemen. Dead, Right Reverends and Wrong Reverends of every order. Dead, men and women, born with Heavenly compassion in your hearts. And dying thus around us every day.'* (Dickens, 1985a, 596)

The charitable projects of the Mrs Jellabys and Mrs Pardiggles of that world were more likely to add to the miseries of the capitalist system than to relieve suffering and injustice. In this period, colonising of the poor via paternalistic philanthropism was the domestic counterpart of overseas empire-building.

Charity in various guises is also a central theme of *Jane Eyre*. At the outset, the heroine lives with the relatives who have taken her in after the death of her parents. However, they view her as a burden, and exploit and torment her. When she opposes their ill-treatment, she is sent to a charity school, which is represented as a cruel, strict, mean establishment, with little food or warmth or freedom for its pupils, to the extent that many die from epidemics. After she flees from Mr Rochester, she is close to starving when she is taken in by two sisters, living in isolation on the moors: here she meets true charity for the first time. A clergyman, brother to her benefactors, finds her a teaching position, and then inveigles her to join his missionary work to India: he offers a stern and self-denying model of Christian service, which she rejects. Finally, she is reunited with the blind and maimed Rochester and takes up a role as wife, nurse, and ultimately mother.

The Christian approach of Charlotte Brontë and Charles Dickens highlights the fact that the injunction to give charity is a religious obligation. Yet their critique of actually existing charity suggests the tension that exists between the motivation to serve God by helping the poorest, and the way in which the social organisation of charity subverts the moral imperative. From the early fourteenth century, there were attempts to organise charitable donations, in order to reduce the problem of vagrancy and prevent malingering by able-bodied labourers. The resulting network of religious organisations, mutal aid societies, friendly societies and philanthropists proved increasingly unable to deal with the diswelfares of unrestrained industrial capitalism.

In the late nineteenth century, various reforms, including the work of the Charity Organization Society, brought about a coordination of voluntary organisations, and also heralded the beginnings of formal social work. As the welfare state developed via the work of Liberals such as Lloyd George and Beveridge, the role of charities changed, but did not necessarily diminish. Symbolically, the institutionalisation of altruism through the organisation of charity remains a model influencing the way help is delivered and understood in the society of the late twentieth-century:

> *'The concept of charity, as refined by the courts, has an underlying social philosophy which has remained intact and has influenced the whole of our society's view of social welfare provision. Running consistently through the decisions is the idea of* "bounty". "Bounty" in the legal context *means more than just liberality. Preserved within it, like a fly in amber, is a concept of social relations in which some people are active agents and others just passive recipients.'* (Williams, 1989, 42)

As the shortfalls and inequities of the postwar welfare state became obvious during the 1960s and 1970s, so a new generation of pressure groups such as Shelter and the Child Poverty Action Group developed to press for social change. Meanwhile, the big disability charities remained major sources of support for large numbers of disabled people.

Since the advent of community care, statutory authorities have increasingly moved to being funding agencies, purchasing the services provided by private and voluntary organisations. Once again, charitable organisations have a key role in providing social welfare: by 1995, two-thirds of voluntary organisations were in receipt of contractual support. Community care was partly introduced as a way of containing public expenditure. Voluntary organisations were favoured over private organisations for a range of reasons such as their not-for-profit ethos, their supposedly higher standards, and possibly also because they could be more easily controlled by local authority social services departments.

Since the 1970s, it is the disability movement, above all, that has continued the traditional critique of charitable hypocrisy which was established by Dickens and his contemporaries. Robert Drake (1996b) has summarised the five major areas where the role of disability charities has been found wanting. First, charities define the problems of their clients in individualist terms, using the medical model of disability. Second, charities speak for disabled people in negotiations with government, monopolise resources and set the priorities for intervention. Third, charities are led by non-disabled people and employ predominantly non-disabled people, are often unresponsive to disabled people or other users, and are hierarchical and undemocratic. Fourth, charities are politically inert: prevented from campaigning by the Charity Commission, they are prevented from working for changes to the law. Fifth and finally, charities have traditionally used exploitative images of disabled people in order to raise money.

With the slogan 'rights not charity', the disability movement has identified the role of charities as a major obstacle to the liberation of disabled people. As the photographer and critic David Hevey has written, '*Charity advertising serves as the calling-card of an inaccessible society which systematically segregates disabled people*' (1992, 24). Images of disabled people as victims of their medical conditions, or as incapable and dependent, reinforce the idea of disabled people as helpless. While charities may claim to be working for the empowerment of disabled people, the continuation of high-profile imagery which undermines the dignity and agency of people with impairments contradicts their intentions. Some charities have begun to change their imagery, and their ways of working, but progress is slow. Only very limited consumer participation is being achieved (Drake, 1996b, 160). When Robert Drake (1996a) interviewed non-disabled people who ran charities in Wales, they tended to see it as natural that voluntary groups should be run by non-disabled people. Disabled people were seen as passive recipients, who were prevented by their physical or mental limitations from taking leadership roles.

Many of these arguments apply more broadly than just in the disability field: only gradually are voluntary organisations for older people beginning to represent their constituency effectively. Although progressive children's charities consult young people properly and involve them in decision-making, many do not. While the best charities have initiated new models of working far in advance of the statutory sector, there are many rather more conservative organisations. In general, a paternalistic model of help predominates, in which the priorities and practices are agreed by people who are not those in need of support. And the very need for charitable assistance may often be due to the shortfall of mainstream provision or the failures of social organisation, as Drake suggests:

'Were disabled people to command incomes and resources through paid work, and were the social and physical environment suitably adapted so as to remove the obstacles that currently deny disabled people their citizenship, what kinds of duties would then remain for the statutory and voluntary services to perform?' (1996b, 163)

Charities are ways of managing and organising altruism: they set a limit to individual obligation, create appropriate roles, and enable effective delivery to those in need. The Jewish philosopher Maimonides favoured forms of charity in which there was anonymity of donor and recipient, because these prevented stigma and indebtedness. Yet the highest place on his 'golden ladder of charity' was reserved for interventions which removed the structural conditions which made people dependent on the generosity of others. In the same way, the disability movement has campaigned for 'rights not charity', in order that barriers to participation might be removed, and disabled people enabled to access the benefits of citizenship which are currently denied

Above all, the fact remains that charity is not a reliable way for delivering help, because the motivation to give is fragile and uncertain. In *The Gift Relationship*, Titmuss (1970) argued strongly in favour of the voluntary blood donor scheme operated in Britain, but the fact remains that only 6 per cent of those eligible donate blood. Even the motivation to provide now, in case one needs help later, is not always effective. And when it comes to more altruistic service, the same picture applies. In Britain, donations to international disaster relief, volunteers for service overseas or at home, the number of households making charitable donations, and particularly the number of young people giving, have all fallen during the 1990s.

Charity is a way for individuals and society to avoid their obligations to remove social barriers and support needy members of the community. It is rooted in religious morality but enables society to evade moral obligations. Often, charitable organisations are neither accountable nor responsive to the people whom they exist to serve, or else those who receive charity pay a high price in terms of self-esteem. As Bickenbach argues, '*Since a recipient of charity is the beneficiary of another's virtue, a virtue denied to the recipient, charity creates a morally asymmetric relationship*' (1993, 197). Charity exemplifies dependency and sustains it. Helping people is the right thing to do. But the ways in which charity is socially institutionalised create a moral asymmetry. Above all, this is because of the absence of equality between those who give and those who receive charity. Charity becomes a necessity in the context of an unequal and disabling society, but this situation creates stigma and undermines self-esteem and status even further. As the Quaker social reformer Joseph Rowntree wrote, '*Charity as ordinarily practised, the charity of endowment, the charity of emotion, the charity which takes the place of justice, creates much of the misery which it relieves, but does not relieve all the misery it creates.*' quoted inVernon, A (1958) *A Quaker Business Man: the life of Joseph Rowntree, 1836–1925* Allen and Unwin, London. The Hebrew word for charity translates as righteousness, or justice: Zygmunt Bauman quotes the Jewish philosopher Emmanuel Levinas, who argued: '*Charity is impossible without justice, but justice without charity is deformed*' (Bauman, 1997, 49).

Social work

Whereas in traditional societies the family and the community were the main sources of support for disabled people, older people, and others requiring help, in modern societies these roles are supplied by a combination of the family, charities, particularly the Church the state and, to an increasing extent, the market. The postwar welfare state led to an institutionalisation of society's caring responsibilities through local authority social services departments, it being recognised that social mobility and the changing family had created the requirement for society as a whole to support people in need. Charities were then regarded as rather inefficient and outdated (although the voluntary sector has experienced a resurgence in its role since the 1960s). However, direct provision by local authorities was replaced by a commissioning role after the

1990 reforms, which gave social services staff responsibility for assessing need and purchasing care in the market, rather than for social casework.

Most of these developments were intended to increase efficiency, to ensure that user needs were met more effectively, and to promote flexibility and responsiveness. Particularly, in the latter years, innovation was designed to promote care in the community, and remove the perverse incentive which caused people to enter residential care because it was the only way to obtain funding to support their needs. It was also designed to replace the previous service-led model with a needs-led model which would be responsive to the individual situation. However, the rhetoric of empowerment, consultation and choice has concealed an ongoing tradition of cash constraint, dependency and dissatisfaction.

The ambiguity in social work between providing personal services and allocating assistance impersonally was identified by Jordan and others long before the advent of community care:

> '*Thus a combination of factors has gradually altered the style and flavour of local authority social work, shifting it away from the personal and towards a more procedural, official approach. This has even influenced the way traditional social work tasks have been performed, placing emphasis on moving clients around or giving them things rather than listening to what they think and sharing their feelings.*' (Jordan, 1979, 140)

The institutionalisation of welfare within the modern state has replaced helping with a bureaucratic proceduralism which often leaves disabled people and others dissatisfied, not least many social workers themselves:

> '*[In social services departments] there is genuine warmth towards the ideals of empowerment. Yet there is also a mechanistic, controlling trend which arises from the specification of assessment procedures, eligibility criteria, budgetary control, and the contract culture.*' (Stevenson and Parsloe, 1993, 59)

In their new role as assessors and managers of care, social work personnel are often involved with fitting need into bureaucratic categories and rationing services, rather than actually meeting expressed need. The tradition of 'fitting the client to the service', and particularly the dissatisfaction of disabled people with the repeated failure of regular reforms, has continued and even increased in the current landscape of community care. Although there is rhetoric about the new system being needs-led rather than service-led, the key determinant is the available budget: self-defined needs are rejected in favour of what is possible and available.

Service users' needs are often seen as different from those of the rest of the population within the prevailing social work philosophy. Service users are seen as requiring more structured lives than the rest of the population, nor are they empowered to make real choices. The choices which are available remain the same limited options: day centres, meals on wheels, homecare, residential care. There is an absence of imaginative alternatives. Employment is not seen as a need, whereas day centres are, contrary to disabled people's wishes. Moreover, the legal rights of disabled people are ignored, in the failure both to record unmet need (Marchant, 1993, 14) and to meet rights under the 1970 Chronically Sick and Disabled Persons Act, and 1986 Disabled Persons Act, which were reinforced, not superseded, by community care legislation (Morris, 1994b).The needs-based approach still supports the interests of social services, despite the good intentions of national community care policy.

Unsurprisingly, various researchers have found considerable dissatisfaction with the assessment process. For example, over one-third of disabled people and carers responding to SCOPE's survey were fairly or very dissatisfied with community care (Lamb and Layzell, 1995). People felt that social workers overlooked their lifestyles or coping systems, matching them against pre-existing criteria. They felt humiliated by the process and said that, because they were coping, they were not a priority. Begum (1994) highlights specific problems in black disabled people achieving appropriate services. Mark Priestley's research in Derbyshire records that disabled people felt under pressure to make less demands on the service and that they had not been fully involved in the assessment, that they felt patronised, and that they thought social workers were more concerned with their own problems than those of the client (1999, 92ff.). It is this context which explains responses from disabled people such as the following, posted to an activist Internet discussion list:

> *'Surely anyone who has been involved in the disability rights movement must realise that Social Services is the engine of oppression of disabled people? Isn't this obvious? These people have been chosen by "the establishment" – the establishment we are battling with – to carry out the establishment's work – the oppression of disabled people – with maximum efficiency. And they do just that. So why is anyone surprised?'*

When I have spoken to disabled people and other services users about the help they receive from local authorities, they have been strongly critical in their views. For example:

'If you dropped a bomb on most social services departments, you'd be doing them a favour in the sense that they could start from scratch and reorganise.'

'Local authorities can develop schemes. But social services is based on the model of dependency and care. They're not going to change.'

'Ideally, local authorities would deliver services. But people have become so disillusioned with the lack of control. They have had to go outside local authorities.'

The institutionalisation of helping through community care often fails those who have a right to expect their needs to be met. Alongside the well-known failures of residential care (inflexible routine, lack of choice, dependence on others, lack of privacy) have to be set the failures of empowerment and participation which are clear from evaluations of community care. The current climate for many service users – older people, people with HIV/AIDS, disabled people and people with learning difficulties or mental health problems – is of minimal services and maximal dependency.

Altruism and dependency
Exploring the ways in which helping fails brings out two themes. The first is the way that the institutionalisation of need undermines the positive motivations which brought about the service in the first place. The large voluntary groups become driven by the requirement to raise funds, to recruit employees, and to compete in the social welfare market-place. The business values which are needed in order to grow and survive organisationally end up subverting the principles which the charities were founded to serve. The campaigning ethos or radical edge is lost. In local authorities, bureaucratic procedure and hierarchical structures distance the managers from service users, and the requirements of the system predominate over those of the citizen. There is a conflict between the ends and those means which are seen to be necessary to achieve those ends: the means become an end in themselves, or else undermine the possibility of a progressive outcome.

A second theme, demonstrated particularly in the one-to-one relations of helping, whether by professionals, volunteers, neighbours, friends or family, is the ambiguities within altruism itself. Whereas helping is positively valued, in practice it can be misdirected, so that the recipient does not benefit. Or else assistance can conceal selfish motives, often unconsciously, of boosting one's own self-esteem at the cost of the person helped. The conspicuous generosity of millionaires, or celebrities turning out for good causes, may ensure fame and approval, just as in some cultures the phenomenon of potlatch, or ritualised giving, is a way of showing status and power. As Maimonides argued, anonymity is essential to true altruism.

The motivations for helping may be questionable. In its protests against television charity spectaculars such as Telethon and Children in Need, the disability movement has promoted the slogan 'Piss on Pity'. Helping motivated by pity is an inferior substitute for social inclusion and citizenship. The aphorist Lichtenberg wrote:

> *'I experience a very unpleasant sensation if anyone takes pity on me, as the word is commonly used. That is why when people are really angry with someone they employ the expression: such a person is to be pitied. This kind of pity is a species of charity, and charity presupposes need on the one side superfluity on the other . . . '*

Inextricably linked with pity is a feeling of superiority towards the other. Being able to feel pity for someone depends on their remaining in a subordinate position. This was the key to traditional attitudes in the former colonies:

> *'Any attempt to "soften" the power of the oppressor in deference to the weakness of the oppressed almost always manifests itself in the form of false generosity; indeed, the attempt never goes beyond this. In order to have the continued opportunity to express their "generosity", the oppressors must perpetuate injustice as well.'* (Freire, 1972, 21)

In his exploration of *Zen and the Art of Helping*, David Brandon (1990) suggests that pity comprises arrogance mixed with sympathy. Good intentions are entangled with feelings of moral superiority, and recipients of help are seen as unequal and inferior. He contrasts this with the more egalitarian motivation of compassion.

Yet it is not always easy to disentangle positive fellow-feeling from more suspect emotions. For example, as social psychologist David Good has pointed out to me, the word 'condescension' has negative connotations in contemporary usage. It suggest looking down at someone, and a mixture of complacency, smugness and superiority. But, in its origins, it seems to have implied a conscious effort to step down from a higher social position, to abandon one's dignity and equalise relations. Neighbourhood activist Tony Gibson suggested to me that the carol about 'Good King Wenceslas' demonstrates this effective kind of condescension.

King Wenceslas shared the experience of the old man gathering fuel. He endured the conditions and went the distance. But maybe most people were unable to come down to the same level as others without letting people know that they were doing so. Perhaps over time, attempts to overcome status distinction have been regarded with increasing suspicion. Hence the word became pejorative. As Nietzsche suggests, ' *"Stooping to" the weak by the self-confident strong is in the end the birth-act of domination and hierachy: the re-forging of difference into inferiority.'* (quoted in Bauman, 1993, 97).

Those who criticise the good intentions of others are often accused of cynicism and bitterness. It is very difficult to combat oppression when it comes in the form of apparent generosity. Yet, while not discounting the possibility of compassion and justice, we are right to be cautious about apparent motivations to social improvement and reform. There is a danger of helpers ignoring the conflict and difficulty involved in supporting those who are socially excluded: Bill Jordan (1979) describes what he calls the pitfalls of conventional helpfulness, meaning the tendency to keep things nice, friendly and sweet, when really they are complex, brutal, bizzare and menacing. He argues for honest self-criticism on the part of the helper, rather than naïve helpfulness. Sometimes a large dose of realism is necessary to overcome the unrealistic expectations of do-goodness.

With emotions of sympathy and generosity, and the urge to improve difficult situations on behalf of the other, comes a tendency towards control. It is tempting to interpret what is best for the person who requires help, a phenomenon perhaps very common in families. Zygmunt Bauman's phrasing of this process will have echoes in many people's upbringing: '*Because I am responsible, and because I do not shirk my responsibility, I must force the Other to submit to what I, in my best conscience, interpret as "her own good"* '(Bauman, 1993, 91). Because a parent or carer or professional feels that they 'know what is best' for a person who needs help and is regarded as less competent to decide, they risk removing autonomy and control from that person. They may be 'acting in the best interests' of the other, or they may bring about an outcome which is undesirable, but either way they have sacrificed the integrity and often the self-esteem of the person they have tried to help. According to Bauman, ' *"Care for the other"; "doing it for the sake of the other", "doing what is best for the other" and similar love motives are now the legitimizing formulae of domination*' (Bauman, 1993, 103).

These contradictions, of course, operate within family relationships, but also within voluntary and statutory services.

Many disabled people can give examples of this process. Margaret, who has had polio and uses a wheelchair, had battled for control with professionals. When her kitchen was adapted, she had a dispute with occupational therapists as to how it should be organised: when she insisted on doing it her way, they threatened not to provide the funding. The same occupational therapists refused to allow her new toilet to be sited at the height that she wanted. As a result, she ended up falling off the seat, and lying helpless on the floor until her assistant arrived. Despite the fact that disabled people are the ones who experience impairment, and are the ones best qualified to make decisions, professionals routinely think that they know best, and try to overrule the choices of service users.

People who aim to provide assistance may face dilemmas when their assumptions or expectations are not fulfilled by the other. This may lead to a recognition of the control that underlies helping. Marcus is someone who has tried to provide assistance and support to homeless people, but found that things have not gone according to his plan. Forced to examine his own motivations, he concluded to me: '*Saying that we can help them is the charitable way of saying that we want to change them, because they are different from us.*' Again, Bauman summarises the outcome:

> '*The Other is recast as my creation; acting on the best of impulses, I have stolen the Other's authority. It is I now who says what the command commands. I have become the Other's plenipotentiary though I myself signed the power of attorney in the Other's name.*' (Bauman, 1993, 91)

David Brandon suggests that this refusal to accept the autonomy of the other is clouded with a mixture of control, caring and power (Brandon, 1990, 26). Yet this state of affairs might originate in the willingness of the helped person to have the helper take on their problems. It may be the expectations of the other, rather than the controlling tendencies of the helper, which leads to the surrender of power. When one feels helpless, it is very tempting to let someone else take over one's problems. Yet at a later stage, when expectations of a solution are not fulfilled, resentment or cynicism can take over. If the helper does succeed, then a cycle of dependency may result, in which the helped person fails to take responsibility for their own life and perhaps ends up feeling resentment.

Yet while helped people can lose their identity in need, helpers may build their identity on self-sacrifice. Figures such as Albert Schweitzer and Mother Teresa become saints and heroes, yet there is a danger in this model. While all caring involves a measure of sacrifice, a drive to help may take pathological forms.

David Brandon suggests that: '*Helping and caring for others can be a very effective way of concealing desperate personal needs*' (1990, 33). Volunteers may become addicted to helping, because of the way that such positively valued activity gives meaning to their own life. But with these psychological rewards comes the danger of feeling superior and self-righteous. To quote Marcus again, '*Helping is a way of feeling more important. Of feeling more significant than the other person because you are in the control role.*'

The pitfalls of generosity are that it reaffirms the other's inferiority, and boosts one's own ego. A superb literary representation of this process comes in Adam Mars-Jones's powerful story, 'The changes of those terrible years' (Mars-Jones, 1992), a first-person description of a man who gives up his job to care for people with AIDS. As the story develops, we become uncomfortably aware that he is not the altruistic and benign helper that he believes himself to be. He is manipulative and controlling. Clues to this slowly mount up:

'*I was changing the flowers on the sick man's bedside table one morning, when without a word of warning he said. "I know what you're doing." He solemnly informed me that I was trying to drive his lover away, so that I could keep him – in some unspecified and barely imaginable way – for myself.*' (Mars-Jones, 1992, 240)

The narrator's tone is sanctimonious and self-congratulatory, and the reader starts to read between the lines – for example, we suspect that volunteers do not stay long because the narrator is insufferable, or does not want rivals. The key moment comes on the last page of the story, with the narrator at another bedside:

'*I said: "Anthony. If you want to fight this thing, I'm right with you. We'll fight it every step of the way. But if you've had enough, don't be ashamed of it." I squeezed the hand I was holding. "I can let you go now."*

*When he spoke, his voice was thick with thrush, and he left long pauses between his phrases, but I could make out clearly what he said. He said "It's not up to you. **Old** man. Where do you get off telling people when they can die? Look at yourself. You've grown fat on other people's misery. With your television modesty, and your obscene birthday parties for corpses. But you're not going to get me." *' (Mars-Jones, 1992, 250)

The narrator has no self-doubt, he dismisses Anthony as feverish. Dramatic irony is generated because we can see through someone who believes they are acting nobly. The story works, because it is both subtle and ambiguous. The same knife-edge distinction between true altruism and self-serving help operates in life as in this story, and the same tendency for people to delude themselves.

It would be wrong to conclude that helping is ultimately impossible, or that positive values, derived through religious impulses, or through commitment to social justice, or to humanism, are inevitably corrupted and ineffective. It is important to be sceptical, but to avoid cynicism or nihilism: helping is difficult, but can succeed. The processes involved are complex and fragile, but the contradictions can be negotiated. In both *Jane Eyre*, and *Our Mutual Friend*, romantic resolution is only possible when the status of the heroine and her lover have been equalised. The positive values of care are enabled in a context of mutual support. Mr Rochester is brought down by the fire which destroys his home, kills his first wife and disables him. Only subsequently are he and Jane able to form a family. The resolution to Lizzie Hexham's story in *Our Mutual Friend* is similar. Like Jane, she refuses to be compromised by a man who is socially superior to her: both flee, rather than become the mistress of the man they love. Again, it is only after Eugene Wrayburn is injured that he is truly united with Lizzie, who both rescues him from the river and nurses him back to health. Again, the man is somehow redeemed and brought to social equality as a result of disaster and rescue, with the consequence of marriage and a happy ending. These texts show an affirmation of Christian values of charity and help, but in the context of moral and social equality in which respect and mutuality replace sympathy and superiority.

The key to social transformation is combining the individual commitment to assistance on the basis of equal moral worth with a broader undertaking to remove the social and political conditions which perpetuate dependency:

> '*True generosity consists precisely in fighting to destroy the causes which nourish false charity. False charity constrains the fearful and subdued, the "rejects of life", to extend their trembling hands. Real generosity lies in striving so that those hands – whether of individuals or entire peoples – need be extended less and less in supplication, so that more and more they become human hands which work, and by working, transform the world.*'
> (Freire, 1972, 21)

What is true for relations between the West and the developing world is just as true for the colonialism which begins at home.

Chapter 4
HELPFUL

Building on the theme of colonialism, this book has explored the impact on those who receive help, the role of helpers, and the process of helping itself. What options are there for understanding and delivering assistance which empowers rather than disables? Abandoning the philosophy of paternalism, dependency and stigma, and replacing it with a discourse of rights, equality and social justice, is the vital first step. But values and principles have to be combined with systems and policies in order to be realised in practice. The first half of this chapter explores the independent living model developed by the disability movement, raises questions about the relevance of the model for those who do not have physical impairments, and considers other limitations. The second half considers other practical and theoretical contributions which may usefully supplement the independent living idea, especially the feminist ethic of care. I will propose that the most effective way forward would combine elements of this new approach to social policy with the innovations of the disabled people's movement. The question of values is as important as the question of rights: both parts of the equation will be needed in order to achieve positive outcomes for those who are excluded and disempowered.

Independent/integrated living
The disabled people's movement has expressed extreme dissatisfaction with the existing provision of care services. For example, Richard Wood, director of the British Council of Disabled People, has written:

> *'Disabled people have never demanded or asked for care! We have sought independent living which means being able to achieve maximum indepen-dence and control over our own lives. The concept of care seems to many disabled people a tool through which others are able to dominate and manage our lives.'* (Wood, 1991, 199)

Independent living is based on a distinction between physical and social depen-dency. Within the traditional model, ëindependent living skills' are about being able to dress oneself or make a cup of tea. Yet this stress on 'doing it for yourself' is unnecessary, and may lead to the prioritisation of unproductive activity. People with impairments can be independent if they are able to employ others to provide the assistance which they need in order to achieve their goals. This means having the money to pay other people to perform personal services, be this driving the car, lifting in and out of bed or wheelchair, making meals or giving toileting and cleaning assistance.

The four key assumptions of independent living are that all human life is of value; anyone, whatever their impairment, is capable of exerting choices; people who are disabled by society's response to their impairment have the right to assert control over their lives; and that disabled people have the right to partici-pate fully in society (d'Aboville, 1995). As Jenny Morris writes, '*Independent living is about both human and civil rights. If disabled people do not have control over the very basic activities of daily living then they cannot hope even to begin to participate in society on an equal basis*' (1993, 162).

No disabled person wants to be institutionalised, or to be dependent on family members or volunteers in order to survive. Sian Vasey writes:

> '*Before getting a care package and relatively flexible personal assistance I would say my life was a panicky wilderness of stifling dependencies and inappropriate support sytems comprising district nurses, Community Service Volunteers, family and friends, and so on, in which survival was my main goal.*' (1996, 86)

Her experiences lead her to conclude that '. . . *disabled people cannot rely on friends and volunteers for the help they need – we must be able to pay for it and be in control of our day-to-day lives and independent of those around us*' (1996, 87). Disabled people want social independence. This equals autonomy and control over one's own life. In the words of Richard Wood: '*For each and every disabled person the words "choice" and "control" are of paramount importance. These are the words, not care, which should underpin all policies and strategies which impinge on our lives*' (Wood, 1991, 202).

The removal of social and environmental barriers and the provision of direct payments and personal assistance schemes is the way to achieve this outcome, not the perpetuation of dependency through traditional welfare services.

The origins of the British independent living model lie in the Independent Living Fund, a public charity intended by the government to provide £5 million for a small number of disabled people to live in the community, but which was eventually wound up in 1992 with a budget of £97 million, supporting 18,000 people. The advent of community care and the eventual legalisation of direct payments to individuals in 1995 have led to a partial shift towards this vision of independent living, in which disabled people are given money directly in order to pay personal assistants (PAs) a proper wage for performing empowering roles in their lives (Morris, 1993). By 1997, there were over 60 personal assis-tance or independent/integrated living schemes in the United Kingdom.

When people are given the choice as to who they want to help them, they do not recruit professionally trained staff. Jenny Morris's research (1993) found that people with real control over employing their PAs preferred to recruit people with little or no qualifications or experiences. People like nurses and former carers had set ideas about how to do things, and were not prepared to listen to the disabled person's experiences or preferences. In some American states, including Colorado, the Medicaid scheme funds attendant services, the US term for personal assistants. But these services have to be delivered by state certified nursing assistants who have received 80 hours of training. Activists such as Laura Hershey (1998) resent this limitation:

> *'Ever since I moved out of my parents' home, I have hired, trained and supervised my own attendants, based on my own needs and preferences. I negotiated schedules and duties with them, and taught them to do things in the ways that worked best for me. Occasionally, a new attendant would try to presume that her method of transferring me into my wheelchair – based on the instruction she had received in some training program – was better than my tried-and-true method. But I could almost always get them to learn the very valuable lesson that just like everyone else, people with disabilities are individuals who have different personalities, different techniques, and different needs.'*

She makes the point that people who use services provided by agencies do not have control over their lives, and have to depend on the organisational timetable. In her experience, there is usually no need for training:

> *'After all, this isn't brain surgery we're talking about. Most attendant services are essentially non-medical maintenance tasks – dressing, bathing, toileting – which most consumers can self-direct. Does a non-disabled person need special training to dress, bathe and feed herself? Of course not. And a person doing this for someone else does not need special training either. She or he only needs to listen to the directions being given* **by the person receiving the service.**' emphasis original (Hershey, 1998)

While lifting safely is obviously an important issue, in general the skills needed are straightforward: sensitivity, dependability, intelligence and a good sense of humour. While personal assistants may not need particular training, it is important to note that disabled people may need support in becoming employers. Issues such as recruitment, management and budgeting are not beyond disabled people, but there is often a need for back-up, which is why many Centres for Integrated Living run support services or peer group networks.

Extending the model

Independent living is a new approach to meeting personal support needs which is radically different from traditional care. For this reason, only a small minority of social services clients are currently using personal assistance schemes. There is low awareness and a lack of information about the direct payments model, which means it is slow to spread beyond a core constituency of disability movement activists. Sometimes, there has been opposition due to ideological differences or vested interests. Some Labour local authorities were slow to implement direct payments, seeing it as a form of privatisation and a threat to democratic control of welfare services. Because independent living involves a transfer of power from professionals to individual disabled people and their supporters, there has been resistance from those workers who may lose status or control and trade union hostility. Yet many enthusiasts argue that not just the vast majority of disabled people, but also other constituencies such as people with learning difficulties, older people, and people with HIV/AIDS, should be able to benefit from the increased autonomy which personal assistance schemes deliver.

UK legislation currently debars people over 65 from receiving direct payments from such schemes. Clearly, one motivation for this restriction was cost. But there is also a perception that older people will be unwilling or unable to have their care needs met via employing their own personal assistants. Current services make the assumption that independence is only for those under 65. For example, Disability Living Allowance is provided for younger disabled people while those over 65 get Attendance Allowance, implying a dependency model. Yet Arber and Ginn (1991) found that older people prefer to stay in their own home and be cared for by someone who does not live there. If they had no spouse, their preference was for formal carers, so that they could be self-sufficient.

Colin Barnes (1997), at the British Council of Disabled People (BCODP) Research Unit, University of Leeds, has explored the response of older people to independent living via a series of focus groups. His study found that on the whole, older people are unfamiliar with the direct payments model, and although critical of local services, are unenthusiastic about employing personal assistants. Partly this arises from their suspicion that any changes to provision might mean a reduction in local services and confusion about what personal assistants mean. Also, some did not want strangers doing personal care and did not want to become employers. Yet older people with experience of personal assistance schemes were more positive: they felt that the administration was no problem at all; they were enthusiastic about the potential of direct payments, particularly for those who lived alone, or in rural areas where services were scarce; they also felt the benefit of not being reliant on family and friends, in terms of exerting control over their life, and being able to avoid helpers who were not congenial. Many wanted to be able to pay relatives or friends and neighbours on a casual basis. None of the participants in the study felt that older people should be excluded from access to direct payments. They wanted direct payments to be an option, not a substitute for services. The research also suggested the need for national and local registers of paid helpers, and for peer support networks.

As with older people, people with learning difficulties can potentially use the personal assistance model. Yet few know about the possibility of direct payments, and implementation has been slow (Holman, 1999) In general, research shows that community-based services for people with learning difficulties are cheaper, and can enable people to develop their capacities and improve their quality of life (Ryan, 1998). While disabled people and older people may require physical help, perhaps emotional support is the priority for those who are physically capable but intellectually or emotionally restricted. Independent living would have the benefits of avoiding the dependency on relatives discussed earlier.

Modifications to the personal assistance model enable it to be used by people with significant intellectual limitations. The legal framework of a trust is a way of meeting employment responsibilities, for example. Service brokerage was first used in British Columbia in Canada in 1976, as an alternative to institutional care, although it is still rarely used in Britain. With the help of service brokers, people with learning difficulties were enabled to take control of the process of identifying their needs and finding ways to meet them. Packages of individual funding enabled the service user to control the money for their personal support. Service brokers can assist people with learning difficulties to use direct payments, particularly in cases where people have high support needs, while reducing the possible risks of exploitation.

For people with mental health issues, the difficulty may be that when symptoms are not a problem, personal assistance is unnecessary, but in episodes of illness, the individual might not be prepared to use the support of others. However, avoiding the care of families may be important when relatives may be implicated in causing the emotional distress. Equally, many people with mental health problems have very unhappy experiences of psychiatry professionals. Yet retaining some measure of control remains a possibility, even in the case of mental illness. For example, people can prepare crisis cards which express their preferences in the event of problems occurring. These may detail who is to be contacted, actions to be taken, drugs to be avoided. A different mechanism enables service users to maintain control of emergency circumstances, based on the same philosophy of choice and empowerment.

The limits to independent living

In the understandable enthusiasm for personal assistance, there is a danger of seeing it as a panacea and overlooking potential drawbacks and problems. Three limitations are explored here: the financial, the political and the practical. While some research suggests that independent living is actually cheaper than traditional services, there is still no definitive answer. While it is undoubtedly more expensive to live in residential accommodation, it may well be that providing effective and high quality personal assistance demands higher payouts by local authorities than the existing pattern of rather inadequate homecare and nursing support.

The danger is that cheap personal assistance schemes rely on the exploitation of the people who are employed to facilitate independence. The reservation that some commentators express about direct payments for independent living is that it marks a return to the era of personal service. Victorian novels unquestioningly assume the provision of servants. There is a history of working-class women and black women servicing middle-class and white households. Hilary Graham (1991) points out that in 1861, 55 per cent of the women in London who were employed worked in personal service. As late as the 1930s, one million women were in service in Britain.

It could be argued that the individual, privatised relationships promoted by the independent living movement risk emulating this tradition. Legally, personal assistants employed to work in the home are classed as 'domestic servants' and as such are excluded from the limits on working hours. Because of high levels of unemployment, people may be driven to accept pay and conditions which are inadequate. While the majority of disabled people pay wages rather higher than the national minimum wage, there is certainly a potential for exploitation as the model is extended. Certainly, most people employed in this way, even if paid well, do not have job security or pension rights. In most personal assistance relationships which I have personally observed, there is an equality of status and mutual respect. However, anecdotes circulate about personal assistants being treated badly in particular cases, and this is undoubtedly a danger of the largely hidden process of personal help. As Ann Brechin argues, good help should be rewarding for both parties (Brechin, 1998, 178). It would be deeply unfortunate if the liberation of disabled people from dependency contributed to the exploitation of another disempowered section of the population.

However, the late twentieth century has seen a massive expansion of the service sector in Britain and other western countries. As women have entered the workforce, pressure on time has led to a reliance on others to provide domestic services such as cleaning and childcare. Inevitably, in some cases this involves exploitation and a return to the servant ethos. But it does not have to. As André Gorz and others have suggested, the tendency of modern capitalism is for productive jobs to be eliminated by continuing automation and efficiencies of scale. If structural unemployment is a growing problem in modern societies, then employing more people in personal support services is a way of redistributing money from those with jobs to those on the periphery of the economy. Perhaps many young people would accept decently paid work as personal assistants for a period before, after or during tertiary education.

A final problem relates to the practicalities of relying on someone else to deliver personal care. For example, Sian Vasey's account of using personal assistance shows that, even when funding is available, it is still laborious to organise an effective care package. Even with a rota of people to help in the morning, the evening and through the day, it is clear that full freedom and autonomy is almost impossible. Particularly, Vasey mentions problems with holidays, and a feeling that it would be difficult for her to move house to another area. Other disabled people have found that, having secured direct payments, accessible accommodation and suitable assistants, they are then effectively trapped, unable to move to another job or another town without losing the support which enables them to live independently. Obviously these difficulties apply to other forms of residential and community care. But in the absence of back-up, they may be particularly difficult for personal assistance users.

For anyone who relies on someone else for intimate physical tasks, there is an element of inextricable difficulty in receiving care, as Kate Cooney has written:

> *'Your carer has to run parts of your body for you. If you insist it is run exactly the way you would have run it, you will be ridiculously demanding. But it still hurts to let go and it's still hard, getting used to the new, circumscribed you – should I ask for that or shouldn't I?'* (Cooney, 1991)

Many may prefer to have help, especially intimate help, to be given by a loving relative, because of the possibility of trust or lack of embarrassment. Others prefer the more impersonal support of strangers. Yet here there may be a problem of confidentiality. In many cities, the same personal assistants often end up working for different disabled people from a small community, and it may be difficult to maintain privacy and prevent gossip. Yet, the experience of

Sian Vasey and many others is that personal assistance, despite continuing limitations, is vastly preferable to their previous lifestyle. Not all disabled people or elderly people will want to take advantage of the independent living model. But it should be a choice which is available to everyone.

Low-intensity support

Personal assistance is not the only alternative model of support available. For those who do not need a full package of personal assistance, or who are not happy with the responsibility of managing their own care package, other options can ensure continued and secure life in the community, and a high degree of control by service users. Also, many older people and disabled people do not qualify for full social services assistance due to resource constraints and targeting, but they may need some assistance.

New approaches to support avoid empowering professionals at the cost of the people they help. They also avoid the traditional dilemma, that services are available on an all-or-nothing basis: rather than waiting till a crisis occurs, and then providing a residential place, these new forms of support are designed to prevent problems occurring and to maximise the coping capacity of the service user. Low-intensity support can prevent matters deteriorating, and can enable people to live independently in their own homes. This might mean local support workers, telephone helplines (important for out of hours), and mutual support among networks of people, involving skill-sharing and social support. The voluntary sector has played a strong role in such developments.

The KeyRing agency in North London is one model of this new service philosophy, which has been designed to meet the needs of people with learning difficulties who require some support. Part-time workers spend 10 – 12 hours a week with members of a small network, and in return get free accommodation and other financial support. This is an economical way of maximising independence and avoiding either institutionalisation or isolation. A network for ten people with learning difficulties can be run for the cost of a single place in residential care.

The Yorkshire-based Home-Link scheme is a housing support service for people with mental health problems. It provides a combination of housing, often in proximity to other service users, together with individual support from Home-Link workers. The helpers are intentionally not mental health professionals, and the help they provide is not professional but practical and social. This might involve help with budgeting and paperwork, or with household maintenance and decorating, or basic companionship and reassurance. Each person might receive up to half a dozen hours of help per month, but everyone also benefits from mutual support, because other mental health survivors are housed nearby, and social activities can be easily arranged. The benefits of this type of scheme are that it supports vulnerable people, reduces levels of anxiety, strengthens their ability to be independent, and reduces isolation: over half of the Home-Link users had experienced an improvement to their mental health. The scheme also eases friction with neighbours and the wider community, frees up the time of professionals, leads to improvement in housing management and reduces dependency.

Another model, developed particularly for people with learning difficulties, builds on the familiar philosophy of advocacy. A 'circle of support' is a group who get together to help an individual with learning difficulties, and get to know the person well, so that they can provide help and advocacy. By recruiting other members of the community, the individual can move beyond dependence on professional help or their immediate family. Helen Sanderson explains the principle:

> '*The family or other people who care about the individual form a circle of support simply by inviting people to join them to focus on the person's future and collaborate to reach her or his goals and dreams. Meetings are held whenever the family or individual needs them, for example, monthly or quarterly. A circle of support is a practical expression of an inclusive community.*' (Sanderson, 1995, 247)

Community members may make commitments to support people with learning difficulties in different ways: John O'Brien and Connie Lyle O'Brien (1995) list the functions of anchor, allies, assistance, association and agendas, meeting needs ranging from physical support to social contact and political campaigning. These models promote new types of relationship, based on equality and mutual aid, which are important building blocks in restoring a sense of community for everyone.

A range of other developments echo some aspects of the schemes discussed. For example, some housing associations are now offering floating support as an alternative to sheltered housing. This offers social contact, advice and other assistance in a flexible format. Elsewhere, people have organised befriending schemes with volunteers. This parallels the way that the HIV/AIDS community have developed the concept of buddies, defined by Dennis Altman as '*people who would act towards strangers, as ethically they would act towards friends*' (Altman, 1994, 38). (The same concept of the 'universal stranger' was central to Titmuss's discussion of *The Gift Relationship*.) It may be preferable for many adults, whether older people, or people with learning difficulties, mental health problems or HIV/AIDS, to have someone to provide companionship and support who is not an immediate family member. All these types of assistance are based around a model of help, not care, and they seek to empower the user, not the helper or professional. Many centre on the promotion of social inclusion. These low-cost support schemes can be complementary to mainstream services, and can greatly reduce the need for residential care, with all the cost and isolation which that involves.

Low-intensity support has implications for the kinds of community in which we live, and also for the role and priorities of professionals. This last point may connect with the emphasis in the disabled people's movement for barrier removal, rather than individually-based therapy, treatment or casework. The disabled activist and writer Vic Finkelstein has argued that we need to replace medicalised ideas about care with the notion of support: *'The critical issue in the provision of "support" is that the individual with the impairment asserts his or her own aspirations by deciding the goals to be attained while others help to accomplish these aims'* (1998, 4). He calls for a new type of community worker or resource consultant, who would provide support to enable people to overcome social and physical barriers to achieve their personal goals.

> *'The real challenge in developing appropriate mainstream community services based on equal opportunities for all, is winning over service users, providers and policy makers to the notion of disentangling appropriate skills located in the training and qualifications of the current caring professions together with the hitherto unknown and neglected skills that may be informed by a support paradigm and repackaging these into new community based professions.'* (Finkelstein, 1998, 14)

The suggestion is that new forms of support, and new forms of helper, may be not only an alternative to independent living but also complementary to it. They represent another option for those seeking integrated, community-based living which maximises the autonomy and quality of life of formerly marginalised individuals.

Feminist ethic of care
Two alternative theoretical models for reforming care are available. One is based on the independent living principles which have been developed by the disabled people's movement. The second is the feminist ethic of care. Both share some criticisms of actually existing care, but offer significantly different strategies for developing new approaches. Disabled writers promote the civil

rights of disabled people, and suggest that independence can be achieved via personal assistance schemes. Feminist writers favour replacing the discourse of rights with the discourse of care, and deconstructing the notion of independence itself. Yet neither perspective has engaged with the other, despite the opportunities this might offer for a more holistic programme of reform. It is my argument that such a dialectic is the way forward. I will suggest that the contribution of the feminist ethic is of particular benefit on the issues of independence and of values.

The feminist ethic of care originated partly in the work of Carol Gilligan, and particularly from her study *In A Different Voice*, which criticised the traditional models of moral development advanced by psychologists such as Lawrence Kohlberg and suggested that women were not morally underdeveloped, but had a different approach to morality. Jean Tronto (1993) summarises three major distinctions between what has been called the 'ethic of rights', and the feminist ëethic of care'. The ethic of care is based on relationships and responsibilities, while the ethic of rights is based on rights and rules. The former emerges from concrete circumstances, rather than formal and abstract situations. Finally, the ethic of care depends on activity, while the ethic of rights depends on principles. Drawing on these differences, feminist philosophers have argued that public discourse needs to draw on the neglected ethic of care, as a balance to the dominant ethic of rights, and they have elaborated the implications of this approach for welfare.

From a disability studies perspective, one could develop some critiques of this approach. For example, there is a tendency in some of this literature to idealise the caring role, and to develop an almost essentialist idea of women as carers (for example in Noddings, 1984). Yet users of care services may well have reason to reject this for reasons outlined earlier: they may feel taken over, spoken for, undermined, disempowered or even neglected and abused by carers. Moreover, the literature on the feminist ethic of care perhaps fails to grasp a key problem, in the challenge to the ethic of rights, which is variously described as patriarchal in essence or in values (Larrabee, 1993), and which dominates within the public sphere. Abstract universals such as equality and justice are criticised, and a feminist ethic based on relationships and responsibilities is offered as an alternative. This may be a step forward in the public sphere, yet in the private sphere where much caring takes place, a disability rights perspective might argue that the fundamental need is for the application of the ethic of rights to the social relationship of care. So, for example, disabled people have promoted the slogan ërights not charity', demanding personal assistance as of right, instead of dependency on care or kindness. As Anita Silvers argues, *'far from vanquishing patriarchal systems, substituting the ethics of caring for the ethics of equality threatens an even more oppressive paternalism'* (1995, 40).

However, more recent writers from the feminist ethic of care position move away from the opposition of care and rights, and also show more understanding of the problems of disempowerment. For example, Sevenhuijsen and others have criticised what she calls ëthe shadow side of virtue' (Sevenhuijsen 1998, 12), meaning the conflict, aggression and ambivalence which is also sometimes present in caring:

> *'Even if care is to a certain extent generated by dependency and attentiveness, the concrete motives in social practices of care cannot always be derived from the urge to protect dependent people from vulnerability. Caring for others can also stem from less noble motives, such as the urge to meddle or to control others.'* (Sevenhuijsen, 1998, 20)

Marilyn Friedman (1993) argues that justice and caring are mutually compatible: close relationships create special vulnerability to harm and abuse, she claims, and justice is relevant to rectification in this case. In her work, and that of others (Tronto, 1993), there has been some progress towards dissolving the false dichotomy of care versus justice. Certainly, one would want to support the argument that care can bring benefits to democratic citizenship, as long as it was also accepted that justice and equality may bring benefits to caring relationships and the private sphere: this, after all, has been a central part of the feminist project.

Whereas disabled people campaign for independence, feminist ethic philosophers promote the notion of interdependence, seeing liberal ideals of autonomy and independence as being irredeemably bound up with a masculine view of people as separate subjects. For example, Sevenhuijsen criticises autonomy and independence as a goal, and the whole idea of ëatomistic individualism':

> *'The ideal of abstract autonomy in fact overlooks what is is that makes care an element of the human condition, i.e. the recognition that all people are vulnerable, dependent and finite, and that we all have to find ways of dealing with this in our daily existence and in the values which guide our individual and collective behaviour.'* (Sevenhuijsen, 1998, 28)

Because women have historically been the care providers, it is suggested that they are less likely to promote an unrealistic view of independence. They realise that a large proportion of people – babies and children, pregnant women, older people, and sick and disabled people – will rely on others in various ways and at various stages. That is to say, over a life cycle, people will variously both receive and provide care: *'Dependence on care should not be seen as something which can suddenly overtake us; rather it should be seen as an integral part of human existance'* (Sevenhuijsen, 1998, 147). Here there is a revisioning of the idea of human nature to include dependence on others as a core concept.

Moreoever, there is an argument in the feminist ethic literature that it is the denial of this basic interdependence which contributes to the devaluing of people who receive care. Joan Tronto highlights the social construction of dependency which undermines and objectifies ëhelpless' people:

> *'Because neediness is conceived as a threat to autonomy, those who have more needs than us appear to be less autonomous, and hence less powerful and less capable. The result is that one way in which we socially construct those who need care is to think of them as pitiful because they require help.'* (Tronto, 1993, 120)

Selma Sevenhuijsen argues along similar lines:

> *'In the ideal of the atomistic individual, the moral subject is primarily expected to pursue autonomy and independence. In this way, vulnerability and dependency easily become separated from the ideal self and localized in, or projected onto others: weak or "needy" people.'* (1998, 57)

The replacement of independence with interdependence challenges the disability movement approach. Disabled people might reply to the feminist ethic writers that while deconstructing independence sounds good in theory, in practice they would prefer schemes which offer them the choice and control which others already take for granted. As Silvers argues, *'social policy that reconciles equality with difference can advance historically subordinated groups but that displacing equality in favor of positional ethics merely reprises the repression of those already marginalized.'* (1995, 31)

Rather than challenging the goal of independence, disabled people want to be empowered to become independent. The crucial move is not just to recognise that everyone has needs, but to break the link between physical and social dependency. While feminist ethic philosophers may see women's dependency as socially constructed, they often retain an essentialist model when it comes to disability, seeing it as arising from particular physical limitations. They fail to deconstruct care. The independent living model argues that independence consists in being able to make choices and exert control over one's life. It does not mean being able to perform particular physical acts. Direct payments and independent living schemes are very direct ways of ensuring that people gain far more independence, and are not disempowered by inappropriate or demeaning care: in contrast, the ethic of care stress on interdependence seems rather idealistic.

Yet the feminist ethic of care is also a valuable correlative to the independent living model. There can be too much stress on independence and autonomy within disability rights discourse. There is a contradiction between the collectivism of the disability movement and the individualism of the proposed solution to care. In America, this tension is less obvious, because the society is based on individual rights and the free market. Yet Gareth Williams (1984) has identified the dangers of promoting solutions which reify normative ideas of independence, rather than recognising the mutual interests and interdependency of human beings. There is also the problem that there will always be disabled people who are not liberated through barrier removal and personal assistance: some impairments are so significant that work, for example, will always be impossible, as Paul Abberley has argued (1996). Having the individual achievement of independence as the sole value and key goal is to reprise the exclusion of this section of the disabled community.

As feminist ethic philosophers point out, the notion of independence is inherited from a liberal tradition which has historically marginalised those who are not male, not adult, and not physically able. Within liberal individualism, people are regarded as fundamentally the same, they are abstracted from their context, they are seen as separate and bounded by their bodies. The people who count are the people who are independent:

> *'In their need, dependent people are therefore seen to constrain others in their own pursuit of individual freedom. As a result, only those who are without need, or without obligation to those with need, are able to achieve full independence and therefore personhood.'* (Hockey and James, 1993, 110)

Many liberal thinkers, for example Rousseau and Adam Smith, have suggested that people who are dependent lose their ability to exercise autonomy and make judgements; some contemporary bioethicists would agree.

The notion of independence, therefore, is problematic. As Jenny Morris argues,

'*In Western industrial societies, this term has commonly been associated with the ability to do things for oneself, to be self-supporting, self-reliant. When physical impairment means that there are things that someone cannot do for themselves, daily living tasks with which they need help, the assumption is that this person is "dependent". And in Western culture, to be dependent is to be subordinate, to be subject to the control of others.*'
(1993, 22ff.)

For this reason, the disability movement response has been to highlight the social environments which render people with impairments disabled, and to call for systems of personal assistance which enable people to live independently. Yet perhaps it would be more effective to challenge the overall liberal tradition of independence and individualism, rather than to claim access to the notion for a particular excluded population.

This is not to argue against barrier removal or personal assistance. Such innovations are essential to create a 'level playing field', in which interdependency can be based on equality and social justice rather than exclusion. Other innovations might include more extensive day care, the recognition of children's rights, and prohibition of discrimination on the grounds of gender, race, disability and sexuality. We might then recognise that we are all dependent on each other, and that disabled people's limitations are not qualitatively different from those of other human beings.

Challenging independence goes against the grain of contemporary social theory. The work of thinkers such as Anthony Giddens and Ulrich Beck argues for the inevitable rise of individualisation, in which concepts such as choice, freedom and negotiation replace the traditional collective rules and shared values, in a world where more and more people live alone. In this account, independence is vital to living: '*In an individualized society each of us must learn, on pain of remaining at a permanent disadvantage, to conceive of him/herself as the central pivot around which life revolves*' (Beck and Beck-Gernsheim, 1995, 40).

Yet perhaps this approach both overstates the degree of change and is complacent about the dangers of unrestrained individualism. After all, many people who live alone also belong to networks, for example lesbian and gay communities, or communities of protest, or youth subcultures. The family is not so much in decline, as in development to a more varied and pluralist set of possibilities (Smart and Neale, 1999). In the modern world, we are more than ever interdependent, despite our assumptions and attitudes. One disabled person suggested to me that the teenager is an effective metaphor for the illusion of independence which now predominates: '*the typical arrogant healthy teenager who thinks he is independent but relies on a whole network of support to carry out his lifestyle . . . shirts ironed,meals cooked, bills and domestic responsibilities sorted, his toilet cleaned . . .and he sees this as independence?*' And of course, it is no coincidence that the image is of a male.

Should we not see the aids and enabling environment which people with impairments require as part of their way of relating to the world as part of their extended self? If a beaver cannot be understood without a dam, then in the same way a person with paraplegia cannot be imagined separately from their wheelchair. Every human requires some form of clothing and footwear to survive, even or especially in the artificial environments in which we now live. Cars seem a vital part of our species' way of life, even if they threaten to destroy the whole ecosytem on which we rely. Many people require mobile phones and pacemakers and insulin injections and everyone requires mass transit systems and the postal service and food distribution. We should not distinguish between those externalities which we all take for granted but without which we cannot operate and the experience of people with impairment who rely on particular aids to conduct their lives.

The feminist ethic approach to independence, alongside the demand for barrier removal and personal assistance, comprises a broader strategy for empowering disabled people. It recognises that dependency is not an exclusive attribute of older people or people with impairments, but is part of being a member of the species: '*While not all people need others' assistance at all times, it is part of the human condition that our autonomy occurs only after a long period of dependence, and that in many regards, we remain dependent upon others throughout our lives*' (Tronto, 1993, 162). Sally French argues that while we are all dependent on each other, disabled people's limitations are often seen as qualitatively different. Despite the way that self-care skills are emphasised for disabled people, everyone in the workplace, for example, requires assistance and support: '*The crucial difference is that able-bodied people's problems are regarded as normal and acceptable, and thus they can ask assistance of each other without feeling guilty or inferior.*' (1993, 46). Yet our ways of speaking obscure the relations of help and exchange which are going on every day: '*When it is said of people that they can take care of themselves, what is usually meant is that such persons can make sure that others will take of them, that they can return every favour with a counter-favour which its considered its equivalent*' (De Swann, 1990, 27).

We need to challenge the philosophy of independence, narrowly understood, and replace it with a demand for negotiated autonomy, based on the inevitable interdependence of modern societies, and including an understanding of the frailty of the human condition: '*In the redefining of childhood, old age and disability lie the seeds of an expanded adulthood, one which admits and indeed values vulnerability as an essential prerequisite for human growth and development*' (Hockey and James, 1993, 183).

It is necessary to recognise the virtue in necessity, because effective helping is a way of giving satisfaction to the one who helps, as well as the one who is helped:

> '*In striving to realize their objectives, human beings are for ever dependent on one another; everyone depends on other people and almost everyone is needed by some others. That is what conveys to people their significance for their fellow human beings and that is where they find the fulfilment of their existence.*' (De Swann, 1990, 21)

Disabled people, in an enabling society, can also have access to this fulfilment, as parents, carers, workers, partners, activists, artists and members of the community, or simply as people who receive the love, help and support of others.

In the end, values

While the first half of this chapter centred on the independent living agenda, the second half has begun to explore broader questions about the values which should inform society and welfare systems. Drawing on the idea of feminist ethic philosophers and some of the practical models for low-intensity support has led to an argument for community and mutuality as a vital component in reforming the ways in which help is both understood and delivered. However, while challenging the individualism of contemporary society and the failure to recognise interdependency, I am not advocating communitarianism. The con temporary British trend towards teaching civic values within a new form of Christian socialism fills me with concern. When Alisdair MacIntyre writes that ëmodern nation-states which masquerade as embodiments of community are always to be resisted' (MacIntyre, 1994, 303), then I am in whole-hearted agreement. For, as he goes on to argue,

> '*The modern nation-state, in whatever guise, is a dangerous and unmanageable institution, presenting itself on the one hand as a bureaucratic supplier of goods and services, which is always about to, but never actually does, give its clients value for money, and on the other as a*

respository of sacred values, which from time to time invites one to lay down one's life on its behalf.' (MacIntyre, 1994, 303)

With MacIntyre (1987), it is localised forms of community, embodying the practice of the Aristotelian virtues and agreement on what constitutes the good, which I would see as a tenuous but desirable solution to some of the problems of contemporary social policy.

To take this approach is to place welfare reform in the wider context of community development, which includes empowerment of those on the margins through unemployment or poverty, or through living in isolated rural areas or run-down outlying estates. New models of economic and community development build mutuality through schemes such as Local Economic Trading Systems (LETS), structures which enable members to help each other but do not impose a relationship on any two people. These types of network break down need into smaller units, and enable people to make small contributions which are nevertheless valuable. Help is not a matter of all or nothing, in terms of either giving or receiving. In this way, feelings of responsibility or obligation do not build up. It is when people get stuck in the role of helper or helped that dependency develops, in the process known as identity spread: people become fixed in their role, which goes on to dominate other aspects of their personality. LETS can avoid this, and also the scope for people to feel virtuous or for recipients to feel grateful.

Experienced community workers Tony Gibson and Andy Gibson have suggested to me that empowering community work, in the end, often comes down to beliefs and values. Do you believe people are capable of understanding, or acting autonomously, taking control of their lives? If you do not, then you will not be able to work for change. There is a very narrow line between respect and valuing and control. Helpers can have all the right words and the right theory, but wrong practice. They may aim to respect but end up controlling. People need a lot of confidence in order not to take control. It takes strength of character to relax and let go, distinguishing between things getting out of hand and things getting out of your hand. For the Gibsons, it comes down to a basic faith in other people's capacity: a gut feeling, or built-in spirit level. While this understanding can be suppressed or distorted or overlaid, it remains a knowledge which can be trusted about what is 'right'.

In the attack on traditional welfare, and particularly the role of charity and of helpers, there is a danger of writing out the role of values and compassion in the provision of help. Perhaps this reflects the cynical spirit of the age, in the same way that the call for independence apes the wide fetishisation of individualism. Yet there is a need to resist cynicism, and concentrate on the values which might offer the possibility of a solution to those problems which have been outlined in this book. Rights are only half the story. Community is a fragile concept, continually undermined both by the values of the market and by the disabling impacts of particularism and disempowering treatments. But that does not mean that it should not be an ideal which is more explicitly a part of social movement politics.

Postmodernism leads some to suggest that ethics no longer operate, and that there are no foundations for morality, only competing value systems. Yet Zygmunt Bauman has demonstrated that the fundamental imperatives still have resonance and validity in the contemporary world. He suggests that post-modern politics should be guided by liberty, difference and solidarity (1997, 207). In the same vein, but working within a feminist tradition, Fiona Williams has set out seven principles of welfare for the new millennium: interdependence, care, intimacy, bodily integrity, identity, transnational welfare and voice. For Joan Tronto, the feminist ethic of care has four elements: attentiveness, responsibility, competence and responsiveness.

These approaches to politics, and particularly to welfare, allow for the diversity of welfare subjects and avoid fetishising independence or normality. Particularly, they replace a paternalistic approach, based on the standpoint of the helper, with an approach which recognises the autonomy of the person who is helped:

> '*Responsiveness suggests a different way to understand the needs of others rather than to put our selves in their position. Instead it suggests that we consider the other's position as that other expresses it.*' (Tronto, 1993, 136)

Putting yourself in someone else's shoes can be a good thing, but only if it is based on *their* testimony – not your projection of what it is like. This approach means recognising the way that helping can harm: '*The moral precept of responsiveness requires that we remain alert to the possibilities for abuse that arise with vulnerability*' (Tronto, 1993, 135). It also necessitates making communication and dialogue a central part of the strategy for help and empowerment.

Refounding welfare in ethical commitment enables a solution based on justice *and* compassion, rights *and* care. Undoubtedly, the first step in any reform must be the removal of the gross obstacles to the inclusion and equality of marginalised people: for example, with civil rights statutes, personal assistance schemes, and accessible housing and public environments. This would establish a ëlevel playing field', in which there was more balance between disabled people and non-disabled people, and dependency was minimised. Yet at this stage, the values of interdependence and the feminist ethic contribute an important dimension to social life. The independent living combination of direct payments and personal assistance cannot solve all the problems. Moreover, the model will never be appropriate for everyone. Many people want to be able to receive care from family and friends, or do not want the stress of employing their own workers, or may not be capable of the negotiation and responsibility which this involves. Disabled people and others still often depend on good will and mutual aid, as all people do. The danger comes when disabled people have no choice and no alternative, and are reliant on unresponsive services or demeaning charity which render them marginalised and dependent. Yet empowered disabled people will achieve a better quality of life in a community in which each recognises their responsibility to the other, rather than a world made up of competing and selfish individuals seeking to maximise their own advantage.

Zygmunt Bauman argues that commitment to the other is a central part of postmodern ethics. Selma Sevenhuijsen promotes the idea of ëcaring solidarity':

> *'The feminist ethic of care points to forms of solidarity in which there is room for difference, and in which we find out what people in particular situations need in order for them to live with dignity. People must be able to count on solidarity because vulnerability and dependency, as we know, are a part of human existence; we need each other's disinterested support at expected and unexpected moments.'* (Sevenhuijsen, 1998, 147)

This notion of caring solidarity may perhaps offer some promise in trying to break down the dichotomy between disabled and non-disabled people, recognising that everyone is variously dependent, that disabled people are themselves often carers, and that society is based on interdependence. It would be overly utopian to expect that solidarity or community could dissolve otherness entirely. A more realistic aim would involve diverse individuals working together, able to continually renegotiate their otherness in a condition of reciprocity.

The problem of individualism is a particularly western legacy. In Africa, for example, a different tradition assumes not separateness, but community. Rather than the Kantian '*I think therefore I am*', John Mbiti has substituted '*I am because we are, and since we are, therefore I am*' (Battle, 1996, 105). This concept is called 'Ubuntu', and suggests not just that people should be treated as ends, rather than as means to an end, but that people are ends in themselves only through the discovery of who they are in others. Ubuntu theology opposes the western tendency to see individual worth in terms of material success – you are what you produce. It stresses that everyone is a 'God carrier', and that to treat others badly is to spit in the face of God, just as the Quaker tradition exorts us to ëlook for that of God in everyone'.

> *'God has created us all to be different in order that we can realise our need of one another. There is an African idiom: "A person is a person through other persons". I learn to be a human being through association with other human beings.' (Battle, 1996, 96)*

This theology explains the role of people like Desmond Tutu in seeking reconciliation with the white minority after the disastrous experience of apartheid. Having argued in this book that imperialism begins at home, perhaps it is appropriate to end with a liberating concept from the continent which has borne the historical brunt of colonialism.

Chapter 5
CONCLUSION

In the performance of help, we take on different and changing roles. Being help recipients and help providers, helpless and helpful are conditions we have all shared, regardless of impairment or age or social situation. Yet the way in which we experience help can be profoundly different. The argument of this book has been that the social relations of help require reformation, so that these differences do not embody dependency and stigma. Change is needed in the way we occupy roles and conceive helping.

Anthony Trollope's satirical novel *The Warden* concerns a charitable institution run by the Anglican Church which becomes highly controversial. Hiram's Hospital had been set up as the result of a fifteenth-century bequest, in order to house twelve destitute retired labourers. The warden of the institution, Septimus Harding, is a benign old clergyman who lives with his youngest daughter and spends more of his time playing his cello than actively looking after anyone. However, the old men are happy with the situation, and particularly appreciate Mr Harding's care. Mr Bold, a radical young reformer, discovering this state of affairs, starts a campaign against what he sees as the manifest injustice that the will is mainly benefiting the warden himself, rather than the twelve recipients of the charity. Supported by *The Jupiter*, a polemical newspaper, he argues that this is typical church corruption, and that all the income from Hiram's investment should go directly to the old men, rather than mostly to Mr Harding.

Many modern controversies are somewhat anticipated by Trollope's plot. Is it better for older people to live in institutions or in the community? Should welfare take the form of providing collective services, or direct payments so that people can buy their own forms of support? The theme of a charity becoming institutionalised, to the extent that it mainly benefits the people it employs rather than the people it helps is very familiar. As modern readers, our sympathies are divided. Mr Harding is presented as a benign and sincere man, who is shocked to discover that he may be benefiting immorally from money intended for others. He acts kindly and honourably throughout, and while he may be said to be rather naïve and other-worldly, most audiences would not judge him harshly. However, Mr Bold is also presented as motivated by honesty and principle. He regrets the difficulty his campaign will cause Mr Harding and his family, but he feels duty-bound to continue his struggle against the religious establishment. The modern reader may consider him stubbornly self-important, not to say priggish and pompous, but his good intentions are not in doubt.

The church authorities, needless to say, do not emerge well from Trollope's representation. Archdeacon Grantly in particular is depicted as reactionary, stubborn and fairly unprincipled. His slippery justifications for the status quo are easily seen as self-serving and elitist. In particular, he is disparaging of the rights and needs of the old men, who, he feels, get as much as they deserve at present, and are ungrateful to expect more. It must be said that the pensioners do not emerge unscathed from Trollope's satire either: the majority are presented as being avaricious and resentful, or else naïve to the point of foolishness.

A key moral episode in the book occurs when Mr Harding's daughter Eleanor visits Mr Bold, to beg him to desist from his campaign. It needs to be noted that not only is the reformer a close friend of Mr Harding himself, but he is also the prospective husband of Eleanor, who is the best friend of his sister. Eleanor's arguments for Mr Bold to stop his action are based on his sense of kinship with the Harding family, and the kindness he feels to Mr Harding, and implicitly the love he has for Eleanor. In response, the reformer, although moved by her arguments, holds fast to his belief that an injustice has occurred and that this must be set right. Despite the human casualties that may result, he is morally bound to resolve the case in favour of the charitable intention behind Hiram's will.

The impasse between Eleanor and Bold could be analysed as an encounter between the ethic of justice and the ethic of care: abstract rights and rules are counterposed to grounded responsibilities and relationships. For Bold, it is justice which matters, notwithstanding the individuals and personalities involved. Eleanor can only see the human beings who will be hurt by the rigid application of principle. In *The Warden*, we are clearly meant to conclude that it is Eleanor who is right. The reformer's campaign will damage Septimus and Eleanor Harding, and probably derail his own relationship with Eleanor. It is implied that, while the church authorities deserve any defeats coming to them, the old men themselves may well not benefit from the results. They will have given up security and well-being for the lure of money, most of which will be eaten up in lawyers' bills. Trollope, however, is writing a sentimental novel, not a political or ethical tract. It is precisely the point of such fictions that the reader is swayed by the moral dilemmas that individuals face when personal relations and public duties conflict. The skill of an author lies in depicting characters in all their complexity and passion, which may sometimes mean that the reader feels sympathy for thoroughly reprehensible figures, and is alienated from those who do good, but are difficult to identify with.

What message, then, should those anxious to see a reform of our society's approach to personal help and care read in *The Warden*? It suggests that changing the status quo is very difficult, and that the debates which are presented are in some ways irreconcilable. Good motives may have bad results, and reform may be derailed or diverted so that the overall situation does not actually improve. Those who thunder most may be more interested in political advantage than in the well-being of those whose cause they espouse. Sometimes change will lead to conflict between the interests of those working in the welfare state and the interests of those whom the welfare state is intended to benefit. Social progress in general will have individual costs in particular. It also suggests that being well-meaning is not always enough. Many people working as professional or voluntary carers are very well-intentioned. Yet they work within a culture of care which fosters dependency and undermines the human rights of those who receive help.

Thus far, *The Warden* seems rather a conservative book – which reminds us that Trollope was the favourite author of the Conservative prime minister, John Major. Yet the scepticism about reform is matched with a serious critique of traditional social institutions (such as the Church). And the view of human nature is not a conservative one, because almost all the participants in the novel are regarded warmly. In particular, love and affection – between Eleanor and John, between Mr Harding and almost everyone – seems to conquer all. In an imperfect world, change is necessary but not always successful: '*Human reality is messy and ambiguous – and so modern decisions, unlike abstract ethical principles, are ambivalent*' (Bauman, 1993, 32). Human beings are flawed, and the social institutions which they devise go wrong and fail. Yet the impetus to love and to help continues.

Helping – or acting as a moral agent – is a difficult process, in which it is not rules but conscience which opens the way forward. What is it to help? It is certainly not to overwhelm, overtake or invade, but it is to strengthen and even, if necessary, to carry for a while. It is a mutual process, in which there is agency not just in giving, but also in receiving. Help is a collaboration, a shared participation in a common enterprise, but it involves a delicate balancing act, just as with all moral action. Bauman provides the image of riding a bicycle, which involves the delicate coordination of mind and eye and hands and feet. Although we may fall off, we get back on and try again.

This book has challenged the traditional morality of help, and criticised the institutions and professions which embody the imperative, but this is by no means to undermine the duty for members of human communities to act ethically, to provide help. Our task is to remove the cultural conditioning which leads us to impose the burdens of stigma on those who are outside what is considered to be the norm, and to challenge the inequality which contaminates the fields of health and welfare. As Bauman himself concludes,

> *'Contrary to one of the most uncritically accepted philosophical axioms, there is no contradiction between the rejection of (or scepticism towards) the ethics of socially conventionalized and rationally "founded" norms, and the insistence that it does matter, and **matter morally**, what we do and from what we desist.'* Emphasis original (Bauman, 1993, 250)

Birds in the Chimney
Julia Darling

in the end
we are all winged birds
caught in chinmeys

crashing around rooms
searching for doors

believing, with our
beating hearts
that somewhere

in a dark hole
there is light

a place where our wings
can find their span
where safety

is open plan
boundaries are all beneath
our feet

we daren't stop flying at the wall
until we drop, exhausted

surrendering to
our pokey rooms, the confines
of rectangular years.

BIBLIOGRAPHY

Abberley, P (1996) 'Work, utopia and impairment', in Barton, L (ed.) *Disability and Society: emerging issues and insights*, Harlow, Longman, pp 61–79

Alderson, P (1993) *Children's Consent to Surgery* Buckingham, Open University Press

Altman, D (1994) *Power and Community: organization and cultural responses to AIDS* London, Taylor and Francis

Arber, S and Ginn, J (1991) *Gender and Later Life* London, Sage

Baldwin, S and Carlisle, J (1994) *Social Support for Disabled Children and their Families*, London, HMSO

Barnes, C (1990) *Cabbage Syndrome: The social construction of dependence* Lewes, Falmer

Barnes, C (1997) Older people's perceptions of direct payments and self-operated support systems', research report for Help the Aged, University of Leeds

Barrett, M and McIntosh, M (1991) *The Anti-Social Family*, London, Verso

Battle, M (1996) 'The ubuntu theology of Desmond Tutu', in Hulley, Leonard, Kretzschmar, Louise and Pato, Luke Lungile (eds.) *Archbishop Tutu: prophetic witness in South Africa* Cape Town, Human and Rousseau, pp 93–105

Bauman, Z (1997) *Postmodernity and its Discontents* Cambridge, Polity

Bauman, Z (1993) *Postmodern Ethics* Cambridge, Polity

Beauvoir, S de (1976) *The Second Sex*, Harmondsworth, Penguin

Beck, U and Beck-Gernsheim, E (1995) *The Normal Chaos of Love* Cambridge, Polity

Begum, N (1996) 'Doctor, doctor . . . .: Disabled women's experience of general practitioners' in J.Morris, (ed.) *Encounters with Strangers: feminism and disability*, London, Women's Press, pp168–93

Begum, N (1994) 'Optimism, pessimism and care management: the impact of community care policies' in Begum, Nasa *et al.*, *Reflections*,London, CCETSW, pp 143–59

Beresford, B. (1994) *Positively Parents: caring for a severely disabled child* HMSO CCETSW, London

Bickenbach, J E (1993) *Physical Disability and Social Policy* Toronto, University of Toronto Press

Blaxter, M (1980) *The Meaning of Disability* London, Heineman

Bloor, M and McIntosh, J (1990) 'Surveillance and concealment: a comparison of techniques of client resistance' in Cunningham-Burley, S and McKeganey, N *Readings in Medical Sociology* London, Routledge, pp 159 – 81

Brandon, D (1990) *Zen and the Art of Helping* Arkana/Penguin, Harmonsworth

Brechin, A (1998) What makes for good care? In Brechin, A., *et al.,* (eds) *Care Matters: concepts, practice and research in health and social care* London, Sage, pp 170 – 87

Brechin, A, Walmsley, J, Kalz, J and Peace, S, (eds.) (1998) *Care Matters: concepts, practice and research in health and social care* London, Sage

Brontë, C (1977) *Jane Eyre* London, Collins

Bytheway, B and Johnson, J (1998) 'The social construction of "carers" ' in Symonds, A and Kelly, A (eds.) *The Social Construction of Community Care* Basingstoke, Macmillan, pp 241 – 53

Clarke, J (1998) 'Coming to terms with culture' paper presented to social Policy Association Conference, University of Lincolnshire and Humbershire

Clarke, J (1999) 'Coming to terms with culture' in Dean, H and Woods, R (eds.) *Social Policy Review II* London, Social Policy Association, pp???

Cooney, K (1991) 'The girl can't help it' *The Guardian*, 2 January

Cotterill, L, Hayes, L, Flynn, M and Sloper, P (1997) 'Reviewing respite services: some lessons from the literature' *Disability and Society* 12(5) pp 775–88

Crinson, I (1998) 'Putting patients first: the continuity of the consumerist discourse in health policy, from the radical right to New Labour' *Critical Social Policy* 18(2), pp. 227–39

d'Aboville, E (1991) 'Social Work in an organisation of disabled people' in Oliver, M (ed.) *Social Work: Disabled People and Disabling Environments* London, Jessica Kingsley, pp 64–85 d'Aboville, E (1995) *Commissioning Independent Living* London, King's Fund

Dalley, G (1988) *Ideologies of Caring* Basingstoke, Macmillan

Dalley, G (1992) *Disability and Social Policy* London, Policy Studies Institute

Davies, C (1998) 'Caregiving, carework and professional care' in Brechin, A, Walmsley, J, Katz, J and Peace, S (eds.) *Care Matters: concepts, practice and research in health and social care* London, Sage, pp 126 – 38

Davis, K (1993) 'The crafting of good clients' in Swain, J *et al., Disabling Barriers, Enabling Environments* Sage, London, pp 197 – 200

David, L (1997) 'Constructing Normalcy: the bell curve, the novel, and the invention of the disabled body in the nineteenth century' in Davis, L J (ed.) *The disability Studies Reader* New York, Routledge, pp 9 – 28

De Swaan, A (1990) *The Management of Normality: critical essays in health and welfare* London, Routledge

Dickens, C (1978) *Nicholas Nickleby* Harmondsworth, Penguin

Dickens, C (1985a) *Our Mutual Friend* London, Penguin

Dickens, C (1985b) *The Old Curiosity Shop* London, Penguin

Dickens, C (1994) *Bleak House* London, Penguin

Donzelot, J (1980) *The Policing of Families* London, Hutchinson

Douglas, M (1966) *Purity and Danger* Harmondsworth, Penguin

Drake, R F (1996a) 'Charities, authority and disabled people: a qualitative study' *Disability and Society* 11(1) pp 5–24

Drake, R F (1996b) 'A critique of the role of the traditional charities' in Barton, L (ed.) *Disability and Society: emerging issues and insights* Harlow, Longman, pp147–166

Ellis, K (1993) *Squaring the Circle: user and carer participation in needs assessment* York, Joseph Rowntree Foundation

Estes, C (1979) *The Ageing Enterprise* New York, Jossey-Bass

Fanon, F (1986) *Black Skin, White Masks* London, Pluto

Fennell, G, Phillipson, C and Evers, H (1988) *The Sociology of Old Age* Milton Keynes, Open University Press

Finklestein, V (1998) 'The biodynamics of disablement?' paper presented at World Health Organisation Disability and Rehabilitation Systems Research Seminar, Harare, Zimbabwe

Firestone, S (1979) *The Dialectic of Sex* London, Women's Press

Flaubert, G (1981) *Madame Bovary* Harmondsworth, Penguin

Fox, N J (1995) 'Postmodern perspectives on care: the vigil and the gift' *Critical Social Policy* 44 (5) pp 107–125

Fraser, W I (1992) 'The professions, knowledge and practice' in Baron, S R and Haldane, J D (eds.) *Community, Normality and Difference* Aberdeen, Aberdeen University Press pp 25–38

Freidson, E (1970) *Profession of Medicine* New York, Harper and Row

Freire, P (1992) *Pedagogy of the Oppressed* Harmondsworth, Penguin

Friedman, M (1993) 'Beyond caring: the de-moralization of gender' in Larrabee, M J (ed.) *An Ethic of Care: feminist and interdisciplinary perspectives* New York, Routledge, pp 258–273

Froggett, L (1996) 'Instrumentalism, knowledge and gender in social work' *Journal of Social Work Practice* 10(2) pp 119–27

Gallagher, H G (1985) *FDR's Splendid Deception* New York, Dodd Mead

Gillman, M, Swain, J and Heyman, B (1997) 'Life history or "case" history: the objectification of people with learning difficulties through the tyranny of professional discourses' *Disability & Society* 12(5) pp 675–94

Gorz, A (1985) *Paths to Paradise: on the liberation from work* London, Pluto.

Graham, H (1991) 'The concept of caring in feminist research' *Sociology* 25 (1) pp 61 – 78

Harris, J (1998) 'Scientific management, bureau-professionalism, new managerialism: the labour process of state social work' *British Journal of Social Work*, 28, pp 839–62

Hartsock, N (1990) 'Foucault on power: a theory for women?' in Nicholson, L (ed.) *Feminism and Postmodernism* London, Routledge

Heaphy, B, Weeks, J and Donovan, C (forthcoming) 'Narratives of care, love and commitment: AIDS/HIV and non-heterosexual family formations' in Aggleton, P, Hart, G and Davies, P (eds.) *AIDS: Family, Culture and*

Community London, Taylor and Francis, pp 67-82

Hershey, L (1998) 'Attendant services must support independence, not agencies' Laura Hershey's Weekly Web Column, HYPERLINK http://ourworld.compuserve.com/homepages/Laura http://ourworld.compuserve.com/homepages/Laura Hershey/

Hevey, D.(1992) *The Creatures Time Forgot* London, Routledge

Hockey, J and James, J (1993) *Growing Up and Growing Old: ageing and dependency in the life course* London, Sage

Holman, A, with Bewley, C (1999) *Funding Freedom 2000: people with learning difficulties using direct payments* London, Values Into Action

Howe, D (1998) Relationship-based thinking and practice in social work, *Journal of Social Work Practice* 12(1) pp 45–56

Hugman, R (1991) *Power in Caring Professions* Basingstoke, Macmillan

Illich, I (1977a) 'Disabling professions, in *Disabling Professions'* Illich, I., Zola, I K, McKnight, J , Caplan, J and Shaiken, H., London, Marion Boyars,pp 11–39

Illich, I (1977b) *Limits to Medicine* Harmondsworth,Penguin

Jordan, B (1979) *Helping in Social Work* London, RKP

Jordanova, L (1989) *Sexual Visions* New York Harvester Wheatsheaf

Kafka, F (1976) *Metamorphosis* London Secker and Warburg

Keith, Lois and Morris, Jenny (1994) 'Easy targets: a disability rights perspective on the "children as carers" debate' *Critical Social Policy* 44(5) pp 36–57

Lamb, B & Layzel, S (1995) *Disabled in Britain: counting on community care* London, SCOPE

Larrabee, M J, (ed.) (1993) *An Ethic of Care: feminist and interdisciplinary perspectives* New York, Routledge

Lawrence, D H (1960) *Lady Chatterley's Lover* Penguin, London

Lee-Treweek, G (1996) 'Emotion work in care assistant work' in James, V and Gabe, J (eds) Health and the sociology of the Emotions Oxford, Blackwell, pp 115–32

Longmore, P K (1987) 'Screening stereotypes, images of disabled people in television and motion pictures' in: Gartner, A and Joe, T (eds.) *Images of the Disabled, Disabling Images* New York, Praeger, pp 65 – 78

MacIntyre, A (1987) *After Virtue* London, Duckworth

MacIntyre, A (1994) 'A partial response to my critics' in Horton, J and Mendus, S (eds.) *After MacIntyre: critical perspectives on the work of Alisdair MacIntyre* Cambridge, Polity, pp 283–304

McKnight, J (1977) 'Professionalised service and disabling help' in Illich, I *et al.*, (eds) *Disabling Professions* Marion Boyars, London, pp 69 – 90

Marchant, Catriona (1993) 'Off the record' *Community Care* 7 October , p 14

Mars-Jones, Adam (1992) *Monopolies of Loss* London, Faber & Faber

Memmi, A (1990) *The Coloniser and the Colonised* London, Earthscan

Morris, J (1991) *Pride Against Prejudice* London, Women's Press

Morris, J (1993) *Independent Lives: community care and disabled people* Basingstoke, Macmillan

Morris, J (1994) *The Shape of Things To Come: user-led social services* London, National Institute for Social Work

Noddings, N (1984) *Caring: a feminine approach to ethics and moral education* Berkeley, University of California Press

Nouwen, H J M (1976) *Reaching Out: the three movements of the spiritual life* Collins, London

O'Brien, J and O'Brien, C L (1995) 'Building better communities: people with learning difficulties and their allies, lessons from the USA' in Philpot, T and Ward, L (1995) *Values and Visions: changing ideas in services for people with learning difficulties* Oxford, Butterworth Heinemann, pp 363 – 76

O'Hear, A (1997) *Beyond Evolution: human nature and the limits of evolutionary explanation* Oxford, Oxford University Press

Oliver, M and Barnes, C (1998) *Disabled People and Social Policy* Harlow, Longman

Oliver, M (1987) *Social Work with Disabled People* Macmillan, Basingstoke

Oliver, M (1989) 'Disability and Dependency: a creation of industrial societies' in Swain, J, Finklestein,V, French, S and Oliver, M (eds) *Disabling Barriers, Enabling Environments* London, Sage, pp 49 – 60

Oliver, M (1990) *The Politics of Disablement* Macmillan, Basingstoke

Oliver, M (1991) 'Speaking out: disabled people and state welfare' in Dalley, G (ed.) *Disability & Social Policy* London, PSI, pp 156-162

Olsen (1996) 'Young carers: challenging the facts and politics of research into children and caring' *Disability & Society* 11(1) pp. 41–54

Olsen, R and Parker, G (1997) 'A response to Aldridge and Becker – "Disability rights and the denial of young carers: the dangers of zero-sum arguments" ' *Critical Social Policy* 17, pp 125–33

Phillipson, C (1989) 'Challenging dependency: towards a new social work with older people' in Langan, M and Lee, P (eds.) *Radical Social Work Today* London, Unwin Hyman, pp 186 – 98

Phillipson, C, Bernard, M and Strang, P (1986) *Dependency and Independency in Later Life* London, Croom Helm

Philpot, T and Ward, L (eds.) (1995) *Values and Visions: changing ideas in services for people with learning difficulties* Oxford, Butterworth Heinemann

Pitkeathley, J (1989) *It's My Duty, Isn't It? The plight of carers in our society* London, Souvenir Press

Plummer, Ken (1995) *Telling Sexual Stories* London, Routledge

Priestley, M (1999) *Disability Policy and Community Care* London, Jessica Kingsley

Qvortrup, J (1990) 'A voice for children in statistical and social accounting: a plea for children's right to be heard' in James, A and Prout, A (eds.) *Constructing and Reconstructing Childhood* London, Falmer, pp 78 – 98

Rutter, S and Seyman, S (1999) *'He'll never join the army': a report on a Down's Syndrome Association survey into attitudes to people with Down's syndrome amongst medical professionals* London, Downs syndrome Association

Ryan, T (1998) *The Cost of Opportunity: purchasing strategies in the housing and support arrangements of people with learning difficulties* London, Values Into Action

Said, E.W (1994) *Culture and Imperialism* London, Vintage

Sanderson, H (1995) 'Self-advocacy and inclusion: supporting people with profound and multiple disabilities' in Philpot, T and Ward, L (1995) *Values and Visions: changing ideas in services for people with learning difficulties*Oxford, Butterworth Heinemann, pp 244 – 61

Sapey, Bob and Hewitt, Nadia (1991) 'The changing context of social work practice' in Oliver, Michael (ed.) *Social Work: Disabled People and Disabling Environments* London, Jessica Kingsley, pp 40-54

Sevenhuijsen, S (1998) *Citizenship and the Ethics of Care: feminist considerations on justice, morality and politics* London, Routledge

Shakespeare, T and Watson, N (1998) 'Theoretical principles in disabled childhood' in Stalker, K and Robinson, C (eds.) *Growing Up with Disability* London, Jessica Kingsley, pp 13 – 27

Shakespeare, T (1999) 'Losing the plot? Discourses of disability and genetics' *Sociology of Health and Illness* 21(5) 669–88

Silvers, A (1995) 'Reconciling equality to difference: caring (f)or justice for people with disabilities' *Hypatia* 10 (1) pp. 30–5

Smart, C and Neale, B (1999) *Family Fragments?* Cambridge, Polity

St Claire, L (1986) 'Mental retardation: impairment or handicap?' *Disability, Handicap and Society*, 1(3) pp 233–244

Stevenson, Olive and Parsloe, Phyllida (1993) *Community Care and Empowerment* York, Joseph Rowntree Foundation

Thomson, R.G (1997) *Extraordinary Bodies* New York, Columbia University Press

Titmuss, R (1970) *The Gift Relationship* London, Allen & Unwin

Titmuss, R (1968) *Commitment to Welfare* London, Allen & Unwin

Townsend, P (1981) 'The structured dependency of the elderly' *Ageing and Society* 1(21) pp 5–28

Tronto, J C (1993) *Moral Boundaries: a political argument for an ethic of care* London, Routledge

Vasey, S (1996) 'The experience of care' in Hales, G.(ed.) *Beyond Disability: towards an enabling society* London,Sage, pp 82–7

Vernon, A (1958) *A Quaker Business Man: the life of Joseph Rowntree, 1936-1925* London, Allen and Unwin

Wald, N *et al.* (1992) 'Antenatal maternal screening for Down's syndrome: results of a demonstration project' *British Medical Journal* 305, pp 391–94

Warnes, A M (1993) 'Being old, old people and the burdens of burden' *Ageing and Society*, 13, pp 297–338

Williams, G (1984) 'The movement for independent living: an evaluation and critique' *Social Science and Medicine* 17(5) pp1000–12

Williams, I (1989) *The Alms Trade: Charities, past, present and future* London, RKP

Wood, R (1991) 'Care of disabled people' in Dalley, G.(ed.) *Disability & Social Policy* London, PSI, pp 199–202

Wuthnow, R (1991) *Acts of Compassion: caring for others and helping ourselves* Princeton, NJ, Princeton University Press

Young, I M (1997) 'Asymmeterical reciprocity: on moral respect, wonder, and enlarged thought' *Constellations* 3(3) pp340–63

Zarb, G and Nadash, P (1994) *Cashing in on independence: comparing the costs and benefits of cash and services* Derby, British Council of Disabled People

Zola, I K (1977) 'Healthism and disabling medicalization' in Illich, I, Zola, I K, McKnight, J, Caplan, J and Shaiken, H., *Disabling Professions* London, Marion Boyars, pp 41–67

Zola, I K (1989) 'Towards the necessary universalizing of a disability policy' *The Milbank Quarterly*, 67(2) pt. 2., pp 401–28